THE

UNCERTAIN

LEGACY

OF CRISIS

THE UNCERTAIN LEGACY OF CRISIS

EUROPEAN FOREIGN POLICY
FACES THE FUTURE

RICHARD YOUNGS

CARNEGIE
EUROPE

Carnegie Endowment for International Peace
1779 Massachusetts Avenue NW
Washington, DC 20036
P+ 202 483 7600
F+ 202 483 1840
CarnegieEndowment.org

The Carnegie Endowment does not take institutional positions on public policy issues; the views represented here are the author's own and do not necessarily reflect the views of Carnegie, its staff, or its trustees.

To order, contact:
Hopkins Fulfillment Service
P.O. Box 50370
Baltimore, MD 21211-4370
P+ 1 800 537 5487 or 1 410 516 6956
F+ 1 410 516 6998

Cover design by Jocelyn Soly
Composition by Oakland Street Publishing
Printed by United Book Press

Library of Congress Cataloging-in-Publication Data

Youngs, Richard, 1968-
  The uncertain legacy of crisis : European foreign policy faces the future / Richard Youngs.
    pages cm
  Includes bibliographical references and index.
    ISBN 978-0-87003-410-7 (cloth) -- ISBN 978-0-87003-409-1 (pbk.) -- ISBN 978-0-87003-414-5 (electronic) 1. European Union countries--Foreign relations--21st century. 2. European Union countries--Economic conditions--21st century. 3. European Union countries--Economic policy. 4. Financial crises--European Union countries. I. Title.

  JZ1570.A5Y68 2013
  341.242'2--dc23

                              2013025265

CONTENTS

FOREWORD   vii

CHAPTER 1
INTRODUCTION   1

CHAPTER 2
MORE THAN AN ECONOMIC CRISIS   9

CHAPTER 3
BOON OR BANE FOR EUROPEAN GLOBAL INFLUENCE? 31

CHAPTER 4
GEOECONOMIC EUROPE   51

CHAPTER 5
ASIA'S PENINSULA?   73

CHAPTER 6
GOODBYE, LIBERAL WORLD ORDER?   97

CHAPTER 7
CONCLUSION: REDESIGNING GLOBAL EUROPE   123

NOTES   141

INDEX   161

ABOUT THE AUTHOR   169

CARNEGIE EUROPE   170

FOREWORD

A decade ago, foreign policy ambition was everywhere in Europe. The European Union (EU) had recovered from the internal rifts caused by the 2003 Iraq war, and great aspirations had grown out of the conviction that such a show of weakness should never happen again.

Ten years later, the optimism is gone. For half a decade now, the EU has been teetering on the verge of economic collapse due to the eurozone crisis. The idea of a more unified foreign policy role for the EU now appears outlandish, even laughable. Worst of all, to many it seems utterly undesirable. Europe's ambition to be a key player in a multipolar, multilateral global order may not be completely dead, but it has been relegated to the lower end of the list of its priorities.

And the EU's agony has an impact outside Europe as well. The way the eurozone crisis plays out is of enormous economic and strategic importance to the EU's partners around the world. In Washington, policymakers worry about the potential implosion of what is still an essential foreign policy partner for the United States. At a time when the map of global power is being redrawn, a weaker and more inward-looking Europe would be of utmost concern.

"The crisis," as everybody calls it now, has been the subject of a great deal of analysis. But so far there has been no systematic attempt to examine its international impact. In this book, Carnegie Senior Associate Richard Youngs offers a unique connection between the crisis and the EU's global presence. In doing so, he uncovers trends that will have a profound impact on the future of the emerging international order.

This is Richard Youngs's first book for Carnegie Europe. Richard joined us in summer 2013 with an established profile as one of the leading scholars of EU affairs. He is uniquely placed to provide this first assessment of the global implications of the eurozone crisis.

As part of offering insightful commentary and policy recommendations under Carnegie's Strategic Europe banner, we have been asking the big questions about Europe's external footprint. By providing essential analysis on the critical issue of the EU's global role in the wake of the eurozone crisis, this book will lift Carnegie Europe's endeavor to a new level. I am proud to publish this welcome and fresh perspective on Europe's rapidly evolving place in the international arena.

—Jan Techau
Director
Carnegie Europe

CHAPTER 1

INTRODUCTION

Beleaguered Europe continues to lurch from one nominally make-or-break summit to another, its crisis neither surpassed nor broken in definitive denouement. It appears to be trapped within "the recurrent end of the unending," to use T. S. Eliot's evocation of nightmarish repetition.[1] Since 2008, the European Union (EU) has largely been in crisis management mode dealing with the eurozone crisis. The short-term imperatives of ensuring the survival of the euro and the wider, political "European project" have been matter enough for EU leaders. Governments claim that as of late 2013, they have calmed the crisis's most turbulent waters; some observers feel the reprieve is only temporary. Whether or not the worst ravages of turmoil return, it is necessary to look beyond the short term and ask what kind of longer-term legacy the crisis will leave for the EU's global standing and the long-emergent dream of a coherent, active European foreign policy.

The eurozone crisis is primarily economic and internal to the European Union. Yet it is nested within, and is in fact a contributing cause of, a deep shift in global power, one in which Europe commands less relative power, and probably less absolute power, than before. Therefore the view common in some European quarters early in the crisis that it is no more than an ephemeral domestic parenthesis looks unsatisfactorily reductionist. Yet this incipient spillover from the domestic dimensions of the crisis to its international ramifications has been unduly neglected. The time is ripe for a reassessment of EU foreign policy in light of the crisis. This book takes on that task. In examining the myriad effects of the eurozone crisis on Europe's relations with the world, it paints a picture of the interconnections between internal European disorder and a reshaped global order. It finds EU foreign policies increasingly squeezed between the imperatives of internal crisis and the birth pangs of a post-Western international order. And it traces how these factors are simultaneously pulling European governments together and pushing them apart.

Given the gravity and bitter politics of the crisis, the EU's pretensions at global shaping now may seem to represent little more than a laughably, even dangerously, outsized ambition. If the EU had to improve its foreign policy game even before the crisis, such a gear change is clearly more urgent today. The gloom cast by the current crisis leaves much commentary feeling like an eschatology of the EU's last days. Europe certainly presents a more furrowed brow to the world: its tonality is more somber. The EU seems to exhibit the confusion and paralysis of an identity crisis. Yet the book ponders whether there are not also some positive effects. Can Europe defy augury and emerge from the crisis better prepared for the new world order? Many writers and diplomats hold a relaxed view that the crisis has not been dramatic in its impact on the EU's global role. In this view, the EU is not being weakened so much as it is gradually becoming a less active, more suburban power—relatively well off, less idealistic and more healthily concerned with looking after its own material well-being.

I chart a middle course between the most pessimistic and sanguine views. Across the different thematic chapters there emerges a counterintuitive observation: most of the negative features of the EU's predicament were deepening even before the crisis erupted, for a range of quite extraneous reasons. If anything, the menace of at least some of these policy shortcomings has been lightly tempered and corrected in the urgency of responding to the crisis. The crisis has had multifaceted, and often multidirectional, effects. It is like a receding malady that leaves at once scarred disfigurement and a cathartic sense of self-betterment. Europe now neither projects outward as quite the noble Elysium nor stands as an entirely befouled wasteland. To borrow from Tennyson: "Though much is taken, much abides."[2]

FIVE CORE QUESTIONS

Building a composite map of the external impact of the crisis, the book address five core questions:

To what extent is the crisis more than an economic challenge? As a starting hypothesis, the crisis must be understood as a political and ideational crisis, not merely an economic matter. Yet differences remain over how to read the political dimensions of the crisis. For now, the core pillars of the "European social model" remain intact. There has been no leap forward to full political union. The integration model has adapted but continues its familiar path of combining supranationalism with intergovernmentalism in its own unique fashion. Incremental reform rather than reinvention is the appropriate metric to measure the impact of the crisis. German power has strengthened but has not been exercised in the form of heavy-handed hegemony. The crisis has not yet rung the death knell for national democracy. At this stage it seems premature to suggest that the EU must return to year zero, to rebuild in a fundamentally different tenor. Europe is Europe yet.

However, many observers detect signs that the crisis has taken the EU to the precipice of a paradigm shift in the whole model of integration. They argue that the crisis warrants a series of fundamental changes: of European economic models; of institutional arrangements; of democratic accountability; of the way in which power is balanced among different member states. Some have called for scenarios to manage immanent disintegration. The EU's cardinal principles risk being wrought asunder. It remains unclear how a deepening of democratic legitimacy within the European Union can be made to enhance recovery and Europe's global competitiveness, rather than being treated as a trade-off against economic imperatives. The old notion of integration moving through a succession of punctuated equilibria may now seem overly sanguine. To their critics, the EU's institutional, economic, and political templates have shown themselves to be fossilized and resistant to change. This anatomy of internal impacts has complex implications for the domestic base that underpins EU foreign policies.

How much will the crisis affect the core indicators of European international influence? A lurking concern is that the eurozone crisis will leave the EU's structural power drastically weakened on the global stage. Many prognostics are gloomy. It is well known that Europe's relative, structural power was in decline prior to the crisis. The crisis has accelerated the long-term downward trends. Additionally, there is evidence that it has undermined the EU's normative appeal around the world. Pessimists fear that the EU's emblematic "power-by-attraction" will emerge from the crisis resoundingly compromised. European soft power is in danger of becoming outdated, a hackneyed talisman for a discredited power. Europe has certainly lost its allure; it no longer struts as an exemplar of a new global politics. It will spend years atoning for its past hubris. Conversely, rising powers are more importunate in their demands of Europe. The message to Europe from the rest of the world has become: "Heal thyself! Stop peddling the causes of your own maladies."

However, aspects of positive opportunity are not entirely absent. A deepening of economic integration brings into focus the overdue unity between member states that will strengthen the EU's presence in global affairs. Before the crisis many in Europe appeared anesthetized to relative decline; few now retain the stupor. Many observers assert that the EU has always advanced through crisis; its present predicament can likewise be expected to provide a spur to the union's global actions. Rather than the crisis playing only negatively outside the union's borders, many insist that it has shown Europe attempting innovative solutions to the broader problem of global economic imbalances. The EU's normative appeal has not been completely eviscerated in some aspects of policy. Multispeed flexibility may even have some advantages in rendering external polices more agile and better able to combine national and European levels of action. The crisis has produced both more convergence and more divergence among member states. While it has widened a breach between surplus and deficit countries on many financial issues, a crisis-enfeebled EU as a whole has structural reasons to pull together to confront a disadvantageous global shift in power. None of this has provided a dramatic moment of progress through crisis, but some cooperative political will has been generated.

What kind of international policies are necessary for the EU effectively to pursue its economic interests? As the crisis puts the stress on very tangible, material interests, European governments have sought to fashion a more effective form of geoeconomics. Domestic austerity has prompted governments to look outward for new sources of growth. They need to deliver material gain from their international economic policies in a more systematic fashion. The challenge is to do so without undermining EU unity, multilateral governance, or the political values that define their global identity. While some progress has been made, member states have struggled to define optimal strategies for advancing European economic interests in the world after the crisis. Traditional concepts of geoeconomics have returned to drive EU external relations. Member states now pursue and often prioritize their own bilateral commercial diplomatic strategies. At the same time, they join forces on other aspects of international economic policies. Attempts to deepen international market liberalization have been offset by initiatives that instrumentalize market access as a tool of political leverage. The cupidity of much state-backed commercial activism risks becoming excessive. The crisis has reinforced an incipient trend toward a more geoeconomic Europe that embraces some welcome but also some rash, ill-considered policy developments.

To what degree does the crisis entail a shift in power between Europe and Asia? One striking legacy of the eurozone crisis will be a redrawn relationship between Europe and Asia. Analysts and writers concur that the EU had underestimated Asia's rise prior to the crisis. It has since moved to correct this oversight. It is negotiating a plethora of trade accords in Asia, seeking new investment opportunities, searching for help in reducing deficit levels, and deepening a number of "strategic partnerships" in the region. Reflecting the EU's belated recognition of Asia's importance, commitments are now forthcoming to inject real substance into initiatives such as the Asia-Europe Meeting. Putative European engagement now looks to go beyond merely economic relations to elaborate at least a modest form of security dialogue and cooperation with Asian countries. Crucially, the interest is no longer limited to China. Questions remain, however. The EU has not entirely overcome the distrust with which many in Asia have traditionally viewed European policies. The EU is palpably struggling to exert influence beyond its immediate periphery. While the crisis has given Asia significantly more influence over Europe, Europe's subjugation to Asia is offset by the mutually conditioning interdependence that has also deepened as a result of the crisis. The aftershock of the euro crisis has rendered EU-Asian relations more important and more balanced. The essential nature of this relationship, however, remains in a state of uncertain definition.

How far does the crisis throw into question basic tenets of the liberal world order? Many analysts doubt that the liberal world order will survive and argue that the euro crisis tips the scales further in favor of zero-sum realpolitik. There is evidence to suggest that a weakened Europe is less able and less willing to push assertively for the spread of liberal values around the globe. A more pliant EU foreign policy is less rigid in its assumed righteousness. Curiously, however, several aspects of the EU's normative policies have strengthened, not weakened, during the crisis. Through a carefully calibrated mix of realpolitik and normative values, the EU has developed a more selective and rationalized form of cooperative-liberal power.

The irony of the crisis is that Europe's own mismanagement has encouraged rising powers in some select areas to become more committed international stakeholders and work with the EU on cooperative problem solving. Most crucially, the reactions of countries outside Europe invite the EU to recast the way in which it seeks to advance liberal values. The union has traditionally sought to encourage other countries to upload EU rules and regulations and to find inspiration and concrete lessons in its own integrative experience. This means of exerting international influence is less pertinent to a postcrisis, reshaped global order. A less vainglorious and hortatory Europe is no bad thing; the question remains whether it is an opening move toward a more sensitive and thus effective global liberalism.

THE ROAD AHEAD

In addressing these five core questions, I assess the two-way linkages between the EU's internal and external crises, with a view to both analytic and policy-relevant insight. Analytically, the twin crises enjoin analysts to reassess their understanding of the relationship between the EU and its wider international context. In policy terms, moving beyond the economic crisis requires a more effective set of external policies. Even if there will be no single-moment end to the crisis, the EU needs an intellectual and policy-oriented map for its geostrategic aftermath. It is vital to assess the implications of the crisis for the manner in which the EU pursues its global interests.

European governments have regularly talked about the need to update the EU's global strategies to deal with the current array of external and internal challenges. The book's final chapter examines the challenges inherent in the EU's quest for a strategic internationalism that is apprised of the severity of the crisis but does not brook undue lassitude in the EU's global ambition. The EU has admirably sought to chart a path between overwrought millenarianism and laconic business as usual. But there are a number of outstanding factors that will determine whether it can indeed fashion a truly effective multipolar internationalism despite its members' conflicting beliefs. The future EU is likely to be less a paladin of old-style normative power and more of a coalition-building entrepreneur. The EU's use of its strategic resources has often been both improvident and prodigal; the challenge for future European foreign policy will be to determine how it can marshal its scarcer resources with greater precision.

In his famous "Prophecy" on Europe's thwarted political dreams, William Blake described a continent confused between division and idealism, its fractured strife "drown'd in shady woe and visionary joy."[3] More than two hundred years later this quixotically split personality has resurfaced, rendered sharper by the economic crisis. The twin-faced dissonance will linger as turmoil's heir. The paradox of the crisis is that halcyon EUlogy and corrosive undoing have both emerged as specters to combat.

CHAPTER 2

MORE THAN
AN ECONOMIC CRISIS

H as the crisis propelled the EU toward fundamental revision and wholesale reinvention, or do such commonly made suggestions constitute a panicky, febrile overreaction to the current economic calumny? To answer this heavily present question, this chapter unpacks three dimensions of Europe's crisis. First, how far it has altered the European Union's economic model. Second, to what extent it has brought the EU to the verge of political union and recast the dynamics of the EU's democratic legitimacy. Third, how far power has shifted between different states and in particular bestowed on Germany unprecedented hegemonic power. Five years into the crisis, it can be hazarded that these three strands together constitute a crisis whose impact is certain to last. Europe has witnessed turmoil that is far more than a routine crisis. Whether it stands on the threshold of an entire paradigm shift remains to be seen.

If and when the sound and fury of the crisis abate, the EU will have changed across these three vectors: its economic policy; the concerns of democratic participation in European decisionmaking; and its internal power balances. For the moment, in each dimension many familiar, longstanding features endure. The EU is still broadly the same beast, recognizable in its strengths and weaknesses, and in its sui generis political structure. Yet the crisis has unleashed forces that raise the prospect of fundamental reordering. Even if the EU precariously begins to climb from the darkest depths of catastrophe, it faces deep-seated, yet-unaddressed, political, economic, and institutional challenges that have roots beyond the euro's design faults and current crisis. By sketching such postcrisis contours, this chapter lays the necessary foundations for examining the precise ways in which the aftershock of the crisis has spread outward to the global level.

HOW MUCH CHANGE IN THE EU'S ECONOMIC MODEL?

For more than five years, day-to-day news has laid bare every twist in the querulous and insidious saga of recession and fiscal austerity. The central question of debate has been whether austerity has been unduly harsh or essential to save the euro. It is undoubtedly the case that reforms have bitten deep, stifled short-term growth, and caused much personal tragedy. A broader and thornier question is whether they have fundamentally changed the EU's economic model—for good or for bad. Standing back from each turn in the high drama of the crisis, it is necessary to assess the fate of the core, underlying features of European social and economic policy.

Since the crisis erupted, there has been much comment about the need to reinvent capitalism. Conventional wisdom now holds that we face not just a deep economic recession but an incipient and necessary move to a whole new economic model. Some experts believe European governments are obliged to make epoch-changing incisions into the continent's vaunted social model. For others, it is the free market foundations of EU integration that are now rightly under scrutiny. Diagnostics of the EU "social market" model differ: some insist it is the first half of this equation (overspending) that has failed, others that the latter part (free markets) has been taken too far. Governments have struggled to redesign both strands of the model.

As is well chronicled, austerity has been harmfully draconian and adjustment imbalanced. Greece has cut expenditure by a margin unprecedented in the history of the Organization for Economic Cooperation and Development (OECD), while its economy has shrunk by a quarter and its labor costs have been sliced by 15 percent. Spain has implemented spending cuts worth a huge 80 billion euros, as well as far-reaching labor reforms; wage cuts have restored half of the loss in competitiveness the country suffered in the decade prior to the crisis. Germany's resistance to transfers though

Eurobonds and large-scale bank bailouts strikes many as a highly constricted stance when its own economic success has benefited so decisively from
consumption-oriented policies in the south of Europe. Experts fear that
austerity measures are now eating into public investment, education, and
research and development to an extent that undermines long-term growth
potential.[1] Governments have not agreed on a large-scale solidarity fund,
and proposals for more far-reaching aspects of economic union have not
been followed through. While the first stages of a possible banking union
are now moving forward, to date Germany has resisted the notion of any
shared European debt mutualization. Economists argue that problems de-
rive from the toxic assets on banks' balance sheets, not Europe's overall
public debt levels. Germany has erred in conflating austerity and reform.
Even the International Monetary Fund (IMF) has come to advocate gen-
tler belt-tightening in Europe. After an initial European stimulus, both
the United States and China are now more growth-oriented than the European Union. Even if the general case for fiscal consolidation is accepted,
research finds that cuts have been implemented in an egregiously regressive
fashion, sharpening inequalities both within and between member states.[2]

Naturally, there is another side to the equation. German Chancellor
Angela Merkel supported the European Central Bank's promise to provide Outright Monetary Transactions against the Bundesbank, in what for
many observers was the key turning point of the crisis. German officials
stress that they have accepted two—and now probably three—de facto
Greek defaults, suffered financial losses, agreed to a rescheduling of several states' debt repayments, and consented to back-loading conditionality.
Aid to Greece has totaled more than 170 percent of the country's GDP,
in excess of any other rescue package in recent history; and the country's
public debt is still on track to be 140 percent of GDP in 2020. Spain won
an extra year to reduce its deficit; at the end of 2012 the EU declared that
the government in Madrid would not need to implement any further austerity measures even though it was by now set to exceed its 2013 deficit
targets by an even larger margin. Even after this, the Spanish government
declared in April 2013 that it would now not seek to meet its deficit target
for an additional two years. The Italian and Spanish governments have
explicitly declared victory over German Chancellor Angela Merkel as they
have retreated from a number of planned labor market reforms. Spending

cuts notwithstanding, Italy has moved very few steps away from a highly corporatist form of capitalism.[3] In spring 2013 Germany accepted a bailout for stricken Cyprus on far more lenient terms than it had initially said were acceptable.

In May 2013 the most significant retreat from austerity occurred when the EU relaxed scheduled cutbacks in seven member states, including France, and steps were taken to release several sources of new EU funds for growth. Changes in Portugal's coalition ministerial lineup took the focus away from austerity in the summer of 2013. The Commission and IMF then released new tranches of aid to Greece and Portugal despite acknowledging that agreed reforms had not been implemented. Deficit trends have returned to an upward trajectory to an extent that has pushed up interest rates.

It remains unclear whether the "fiscal compact" agreed to in 2011 will actually lead to member states invoking legal sanctions against deficit-incurring governments. The conditionality on financial support faced by European governments remains much weaker than what the EU imposed on developing economies during many years. By 2012 most European rhetoric was focusing on the need for growth. At the crucial June 2012 summit, leaders agreed to a 120 billion euro package for "fast-acting growth measures." Sebastian Mallaby insists that the degree of demand-stimulating, system-saving intervention has in fact been mind-boggling, including on the part of a European Central Bank previously neuralgic about such operations.[4] Martin Wolf saw the EU heading toward a combination of an "insurance union" with an "adjustment union": shared insurance against serious shocks and crises, accompanied by mechanisms to guarantee adjustments.[5]

Whether one believes austerity to have been necessary and overdue or counterproductive and gratuitously demeaning, it is not clear that a fundamentally altered European political economy has yet risen from its wake. Even after the ravages of crisis cutbacks, Europe still accounts for 60 percent of global spending on social protection. EU governments' spending on social protection has increased since 2007 from 26 percent of GDP to 29 percent. Moreover, the margin by which the size of the European state exceeds that in other regions, including the United States, East Asia, and Latin America, has widened in recent years.[6] France's state has continued to expand, accounting for 57 percent of GDP by 2013. François Hollande's economic policy has centered on state-backed reindustrialization and the threat of tariffs against rising powers for not increasing European-style social spending.

Detailed academic studies conclude that, despite the raft of austerity-driven reforms, a remarkable continuity is evident in the institutional patterns, or "coordination modes," of member states' different models of capitalism.[7] For all the talk of "state capitalism" taking shape in the developing world as a challenge to Western liberalism, government now assumes a larger share of the economy in Europe than in any other region.[8] Trends resonate with German-style *Ordnungspolitik*. It might be suggested that the crisis has tilted preferences back in favor of the continental "coordinated market economy" variety of capitalism. Steven Hill optimistically insists that the crisis actually validates the EU's "social capitalism," which he argues emerges relegitimized compared with both U.S. neoliberalism and Asian economic strategies.[9] The notion of state and market working together may seem like a new departure to some in Britain, but on the continent it cannot be said to represent a qualitatively remodeled form of capitalism.[10] For all the polarization of the crisis, a consensus persists around "social-" or "reform-liberalism."

Luminaries such as Joseph Stiglitz and Robert Skidelsky lament that "market fundamentalism" overturned a fleeting moment of Keynesian breakthrough.[11] Others see a form of more regulated capitalism taking shape; by early 2013, nearly fifty new EU financial regulations were in the pipeline, and regulatory controls played a large part in dramatically reducing the 2012 profits of Britain's largest banks.[12] The irony of the crisis is that the state "is back" and being denuded of resources at the same time. Both things are happening together: efforts to boost regulation to correct and contain the market, but also orthodoxy in fiscal austerity. The state will have less to spend, so interventionism based on spending will be thinner, but there will be more intrusive regulation and financial monitoring. In practice, however, financial regulation has not been stiffened enough meaningfully to change the balance of power between state and market. Other than in its capping of bankers' bonuses, the EU has done little fundamentally to challenge the U.S.-oriented liberal model of global financial regulation. In defiance of initial predictions, the crisis has not heralded the end of an era for the banks: regulations have not terminated the insidious excesses of proprietary banking. After a first flush of new restrictions, the technical bodies of financial regulation have put the brakes on the extent of reform. This club-like world of vested interests has succeeded in resisting far-reaching change.

Beyond the "more versus less austerity" debate, the most worrying doubt is whether responses to the crisis have equipped the EU to deal with the longer-term challenges of global competitiveness and sustainability. The tightening of control over deficits, fiscal policies, and banking regulation have all been sanctioned through ad hoc intergovernmental accords, not a comprehensively designed or strategically focused new "economic government."[13] Problems intrinsic to the euro are crowding out those inherent in Europe's poor competitiveness. The "growth" discourse in some senses displaces the problem, in that it merely invites the question of what generates growth. The overwhelming focus on debating different shades of austerity has diverted attention from the changes needed for the EU political economy to meet such underlying challenges.

Progress has been registered in addressing the European economy's underlying challenges. Some economists suggest that the crisis has in fact spurred structural reform and a search for competitiveness that would otherwise not have materialized, and which will eventually leave Europe much stronger.[14] A report by Allianz Consulting at the end of 2012 concluded that competitiveness gains are already improving current accounts in "peripheral" member states, while Germany is beginning to accept a modicum of wage inflation, heralding the long overdue rebalancing of the eurozone economy.[15] In 2012 the Netherlands climbed back up into the top five of global competitive states, after a series of structural reforms. Nordic states have weathered the crisis well because they have already reduced debt levels and made their vaunted states more efficient, actually widening the space available to retain welfare provision. In recent decades many developing states have recovered from banking and fiscal crises without long-term damage; even if Europe's underlying problems are rather more serious than those of the United States, this is a lesson that augurs well.[16] Some observers insist that most non-Western economies have recently risen on the basis of a commodity bubble that is unlikely to endure, while many European economies have been quietly tackling underlying, long-term reforms.[17]

Policymakers have begun to turn their attention back to the competitiveness-oriented EU2020 *Strategy for Smart, Sustainable and Inclusive Growth* and intimate that this will form the focus of a next stage of conditionalities. Conditions on southern states have moved from nominal targets to reform commitments. Talk has emerged of a more concerted policy for investment and competitiveness, in particular harnessing European Investment Bank support. Ideas have been put forward for financial rewards to be given to member states specifically for competitiveness measures. In a detailed survey, the *Economist* reports that the crisis has jolted European governments into launching a battery of new initiatives to assist innovators and entrepreneurs, even if many of them are still embryonic.[18] In 2012 the EU budget for measures to enhance competitiveness rose by 10 percent.[19] Overall research expenditure in the union increased in 2011–2012 to 2 percent of GDP, even if this remains well short of the 3 percent target set by the 2020 strategy.[20] A number of governments have finally agreed to a common European patent system, which is scheduled to come into force in 2014. The measure is as vital as it is overdue, given that four times as many patents are registered per person in the United States as in Europe. François Hollande has launched a 20 billion euro competitive initiative to shake up French companies.[21] And in response to stubbornly declining competitiveness indicators, his government launched an extensive new industrial strategy in September 2013, which promised to mix a focus on entrepreneurship with pressure on the European Commission to facilitate the creation of European champions in the global marketplace.

However, many other measures have headed in the wrong direction. A focus on large-scale infrastructure as a supposed panacea fails to identify Europe's real needs. Europe produces only a fifth of the number of engineers that China and India produce each year. The most pressing problem is the paucity of venture capital in Europe compared with other regions, not a shortage of big infrastructure projects that may just add more unused high-speed trains and motorways in places such as Spain that helped run up astronomical debt levels in the first place.[22] In February 2012, eleven member states signed a letter on completing the single market to rejuvenate market competitiveness; France and Germany declined to sign. Europe is most lacking in producing "Yollies," as young leading innovators are known. Its productivity has improved but in established sectors rather than in sectors that are new and innovation-based. The EU needs talent, arguably more than it needs classic large-scale public works. Yet since the crisis, member states are making it more difficult for research students to stay and work in Europe. Talent now heads toward Asia and, still, the United States; and, indeed, increasingly out of Europe.

The disconnect between science and business is an associated weak spot.[23] One generally positive European Commission report laments that the EU's innovation policy has been particularly "slow and ineffective," overly bureaucratic, limited in both quantitative and qualitative terms, and "too narrowly European." The much-trumpeted Innovation Union initiative launched in 2010 has failed to achieve any tangible change of approach.[24] One eminent economist laments the particularly pernicious effects of the current policy mix of both cutting deficits and throwing money at big projects: new initiatives have merely replicated the Structural Funds, whose infrastructure initiatives have still not been embedded in an underlying program of productivity gain, through better education, improving the investment climate, and focusing on niche areas.[25] Reforms have failed significantly to move spending away from transfer payments to competitiveness-enhancing investment.

Europe's most respected economists fear a long-term fragmentation and divergence of competitiveness and economic outlook—both between eurozone ins and outs, and between north and south within the eurozone itself.[26] Senior OECD figures worry that the EU still lacks the core adaptability required to deal successfully with the reshaped world order. Experts in Spain argue that far more than labor market liberalization is required to establish a firm basis for enhanced competitiveness and growth: the political class has resisted any prizing apart of state and economy to reduce "state capture"; historically rooted rentier capitalism persists; and Spain requires growth generated by more venture capital, measures to facilitate entrepreneurship, and a reversal of crisis-related cuts to research and development.[27]

The pertinent question is not of more or less regulation per se, but the need for more of the right types of regulation and less of the wrong types. Europe's problem is not the overall level of spending, but the orientation of expenditure to current account obligations rather than competitiveness-enhancing investment. The share of investment in overall GDP in China is nearly three times as high as in Europe. In this sense, critics berate the EU for now expecting too much of supply-side reform, when the lack of attention to stimulating and rebalancing demand across different national economies is itself holding back the kind of investment that enhances competitiveness.[28] Some fear that as the markets have calmed during the latter part of 2013, the perception that member states can grow their way out of the crisis without far-reaching reform has taken firmer hold. Pessimists insist that improvements in economic indicators in late 2013 were more cyclical than structural, and that crisis will soon return.[29]

Roger Liddle argues that the commission needs to promote growth more strategically, in particular by providing better support to the most innovative small- and medium-size enterprises, not backing big national champions.[30] EU funds need to be better targeted and not thrown unthinkingly at quick-impact projects. For example, they could cover an employer's costs to incentivize the creation of new jobs. The World Bank claims a strong statistical correlation between overspending on big state projects and Europe's slower growth rates; it argues that state spending has been thrown indiscriminately at Europe's economic problems, massively crowding out private innovation rather than catalyzing it.[31] France has perversely insisted that spending on agriculture be increased in the post-2014 EU budget, while funds have still not been transferred to member states to help meet the aims of the 2020 competitiveness agenda.[32] By late 2013, Enrico Letta was winning plaudits for stabilizing Italy's deficit, but observers point out that his government has done little to attack the structural iniquities of a system upon which politicians themselves depend—indeed, it has launched a number of economic initiatives protecting big Italian conglomerates from outside competition.

Some of the most prominent writers on European political economy have despaired at these trends. Anthony Giddens laments that less support is provided in Europe to assist in worker mobility and retraining than in most rising powers, as funds are consumed by remedial, distributive cover.[33] Philip Cerny argues that while the crisis warrants stronger state regulation, a more "concerted capitalism" or social liberalism also requires regulators to stop merely "fighting the last war" and instead look ahead for new patterns of wealth accumulation.[34] Respected energy experts such as Dieter Helm and Tim Jackson admonish governments for focusing merely on returning to consumption-fueled growth by any means possible with little thought of qualitative change to the economic model, in a climate-induced context that will unavoidably require lower growth over the longer term.[35] One extensive EU consortium argues that short-term crisis management has undermined the move to a new development model, in particular because it has debilitated the quality of human capital.[36] Political philosopher John Gray suggests that today Keynes would not simply be advocating standard demand-stimulating growth but rather ideas "about how we can enjoy a good life in conditions of low growth."[37] These reflections are persuasive, yet are still not firmly encased within the set of EU responses to the crisis.

POLITICAL UNION AND DEMOCRATIC LEGITIMACY

The political dilemmas of the economic crisis have been no less searching. In the midst of the crisis, proposals for federal political union have returned to the agenda. A gradation is widely assumed, leading inexorably from banking to fiscal to economic to political union. The argument has increasingly been aired that a steady-state combination of supranationalism and intergovernmentalism is no longer possible; the result of the crisis is that the EU must either deepen or unravel. The fear stalking strategic deliberation is that the crisis will engender institutional splintering and a more instrumental spirit of intergovernmentalism. The narrative is now of the EU being stranded halfway across a proverbial and roiling stream.

The apparent momentum behind calls for political union derives from concerns over the impact of the crisis on democratic legitimacy. A whole series of more intrusive commitments have taken shape at the European level through an ad hoc accumulation of new roles played by member state deals, the European Central Bank, and the commission, all with little or no matching democratic oversight. The June 2012 bailout deal raises serious questions: the agreement that banks can receive funds directly has had to be implemented in a way that circumvents treaty change and democratic accountability. The ECB's growing role has engendered further concern. Mismanagement of the Cyprus bailout in 2013 most starkly revealed the folly of riding roughshod over popular will. Colin Crouch contends that the encroaching phenomenon of "post-democracy" has been compounded by the financial crisis, as economic responses have further deepened the tutelage of economic elites over popular accountability.[38]

In 2012 the commission produced a blueprint explicitly advocating a political union based on enhanced powers for the European Parliament and European Court of Justice. A report produced under the auspices of European Council President Herman Van Rompuy at the end of 2012 also formally laid out plans for a political union. In this report and in other suggested templates, the main focus for enhancing democratic control has been on boosting the powers of the European Parliament or adding to the latter a chamber of national parliamentarians. Other ideas debated include authorizing the European Parliament to select a combined post of council and commission president; selecting commissioners from among members of the European Parliament; creating a new forum in which the heads of national parliaments' budget committees would meet to monitor budget limits; and having commissioners appear at hearings in national parliaments.[39] A report launched by eleven foreign ministers in September 2012 advocated a familiar array of institutional options, such as a directly elected president of the European Commission and a "two-chamber parliament for Europe" based on the existing European Parliament and the Council of Ministers.

Notwithstanding all these initiatives, in practice no qualitative step forward in political integration has been taken—at least not yet. Leaders chose not to endorse either the commission's blueprint for political union or the Van Rompuy report. In part this is because ad hoc crisis management measures seem to have dragged the eurozone back from the precipice, making political union appear less urgent. As of late 2013 the consensus among diplomats is that there is little prospect of a political union treaty, as the euro's predicament appears to have subsided. After the June 2013 EU summit, even full banking union appeared to be off the agenda. Angela Merkel's reelection in Germany's federal elections of September 2013 is likely to further dampen pressure for political union. The frequent call has been for targeted crisis management not to get caught up in drawn-out steps toward deeper political union.[40] In addition, however, it has become apparent that political union means different things to different member states.

Disagreement exists, for example, on whether the rationale for political union would be to control the periphery or draw resources away from the center. Positions also vary on whether institutional processes should be fully supranational or confederal. The French notion is of a powerful *dirigiste* political system to mobilize state resources; the German concern is with the strict application of law and objectives rules, as enshrined in the country's constitution; the Nordic states and Britain retain more civic-oriented concepts of polity. The German logic for political union is not about enhanced citizen participation but increasing (northern) governments' control over EU budgets. Germany sees political union as a means of tightening existing rules; southern states see it as a means of challenging these same rules. The German model is to take certain monetary rules out of the sphere of political debate—to *de*politicize rather than *re*politicize. Legitimacy looks entirely different from the perspective of the north than it does from the south. Indeed, it may be that Germany's view of political union is a route to delegitimizing the EU in other member states, quite the opposite of restoring democratic credibility.[41] Angela Merkel's speech in the European Parliament in November 2012 stressed the role of member state governments and ad hoc processes outside the scope of the EU institutions in controlling spending.

French officials are less than entirely clear about political union. Their discourse is still sovereigntist, elitist, and eager to avoid lengthy treaty changes and referenda. While for the UK, legitimacy seems to entail fewer rules, French officials insist that for French people legitimacy is a question of more rules being needed to protect individuals from free markets. In the summer of 2013, French ministers rounded on the prospect of supranational Commission interference in domestic policy, in particular as the latter came to focus on France's own weaknesses, not just those of peripheral states. The French elite may have come up against the limit of its traditional postwar strategy: centralizing powers to the EU level was a means of enhancing an étatist spirit that actually strengthened the French state and national interest; now, a bigger further step forward in integration risks rupturing this logic, with the EU level undercutting the French state and power mobilization.

The German constitution and French public opinion are both onerous barriers to a full centralization of political power. Additionally, the UK's threat to use a new treaty to repatriate power has made other member states even more reluctant to embark on a new political union convention.

The proposals for political union that have been forwarded so far consist of somewhat formulaic, institutional reconfigurations, not ideas for fundamentally revitalizing the spirit of European democracy. The focus on strengthening bottom-up, deliberative, and open participatory dynamics remains limited. Politicians often pay lip service to the need for more meaningful citizen engagement. Some insist that the crisis has begun to engender more of a Europeanized political sphere, for example, as countries follow each other's elections with a lot more interest, knowing that the implications of each national vote will rumble across the continent. José Manuel Barroso's 2012 state of the union speech advocated political union but also recognized that this presupposed a more open European political space and civic participation. The European Commission's Global Europe 2050 report argues that a more "open European society" is a prerequisite for a "European renaissance."[42] But in practice, little has been done to flesh out such proclamations with substance.

While a battery of new pan-European civil society initiatives has emerged due to the crisis, they remain limited in scope. Talk of more "flexible" integration has often been reduced to "dealing with the British problem" rather than a means of achieving more effective pan-European engagement. The Lisbon Treaty has removed the principle of subsidiarity. The European Citizens' Initiative became available in April 2012, but social movements dismiss its relevance, especially because of the requirement to gather 1 million signatures for any petition.[43] Hugo Brady astutely contrasts the lack of support for organized civil liberties forums in Europe with the vibrancy of such initiatives in the United States.[44]

An exhaustive mapping of crisis-induced social movements finds that they see the EU as a problem rather than a site of potential solution. Talk of political union is almost the antithesis of the "horizontality" that defines and motivates these groupings, as the EU has failed to present itself as "a creative space to reimagine democracy."[45] One expert observes that the current approach reflects a long-standing continental tradition of conceiving democratic politics as a means to a particular end, rather than embracing the "untidiness" of liberalism as an ethos.[46] Many analysts still present the dilemma primarily in terms of the age-old division between intergovernmentalism and supranationalism, providing two alternative routes of in-direct and direct legitimacy, not as a challenge of qualitative rethinking.[47] Debate has long raged on the lack of a "European political space"; even be-fore the crisis, Vivien Schmidt famously noted the phenomenon of "policy without politics."[48] But experts note that little has been done to foster the conditions for a broader European public space, through generating media awareness and framing EU issues at the national level.[49] Radicals lament that the protests have been driven mainly by the middle class defending entitlements as opposed to a genuinely emancipatory politics. Problemati-cally for the EU, the most acute challenge to elites' suffocation of democ-racy comes from nationalistically rooted conservative-populist movements or indeed the dystopian UK riots of 2011.[50] Ivan Krastev's skillful analysis is that social mobilization against governments is in part a healthy trend but is worryingly devoid of aggregated, coherent alternative visions that can be filtered through representative institutions.[51]

European governments have, in short, declined to explore any innova-tive or ambitious ways of addressing democracy's postcrisis malaise. EU debates seem decidedly out of sync with calls for new forms of account-ability based on participation and associative dynamics. A large number of the most preeminent theorists concur that injecting "democracy" into the union would be different from institutional forms of the nation-state and must be predicated on looser, cosmopolitan networks of participation.[52] A more open-ended and pluralistic process of deliberative dynamism is invited by the need to recognize a growing diversity of opinion over the problem of legitimacy. While civic engagement must be fostered at a Eu-ropean level, the diversity revealed by the crisis means that the legitimacy of national level process, rights, and values must be taken seriously.[53] Some academics feel that convergent values and cross-border communication mean that the bases of a common European public sphere are already in place.[54] But because of the antipathies on display during the crisis, the climb to broadly agreed-upon European rules of the game must be steeper. Young people in different member states have grown into political matu-rity with fundamentally different perspectives on what the EU means for their own interests. If anything, most citizen-based initiatives that have sprung up during the crisis are even more firmly rooted within nationally specific debates.

The "Monnet method" of the precooked fait accompli must now be dead; the economic crisis has killed the permissive consensus that enabled elite-driven centralization. It is necessary to think in terms beyond a formal institutional, democratic deficit. It is time to think of the need to boost accountability against concrete deliverables rather than policies being loosely justified as contributing to deeper integration.[55] The lingering elitism in federalist visions rubs uneasily against the sociological dispersal of power.[56] This impinges on national-level democratic vitality, too. In southern member states there is a nebulous hope that political union will circumvent domestic institutional weaknesses. That is given as the reason, at least, for outweighing governments' determination to resolve those shortcomings at the national level. Representatives of the Hungarian government insist that legitimacy failures at the EU level explain why the Viktor Orban administration won a mandate for overhauling the constitution—instituting changes that drew rebukes from Human Rights Watch and the EU itself.

Debate over democratic legitimacy has been back-to-front: the prevalent official notion is of making sure that agreements on economic policies are implemented, rather than letting democratic debate itself determine those economic choices. Current proposals foreclose discussion over fundamental economic identity; debate instead is reduced to an apparent choice between strengthening the European Parliament and giving greater say to national parliaments. This is a decidedly narrow means of defining democracy enhancement. It is also highly instrumental: proponents favor one or the other in part on the basis of whether they consider the European Parliament or their national parliament more likely to further their particular substantive preferences. In fact, the European Parliament does not offer substantive and adversarial options but still acts as a lobbyist for greater integration and its own rights. Far broader, participative debate is needed: introducing firmer rules may make sense, but only when such a move rests on a strong degree of prior social—not merely elite—consensus. In the United States, the crisis of democracy is one of polarization; in Europe, it is one of frustration with elite consensus politics providing no real alternatives. Absent broader civic engagement, a federal union that springs from the loins of failure risks aggravating the dearth of legitimacy.

It is important not to exaggerate. The predicament is not so much that democracy is on its last legs as it is of managing the divergence in what citizens demand. Party systems have not entirely imploded, and populist parties remain confined within certain margins. Radical nationalists have enjoyed really major success only in Hungary and Greece. In Italy, for all of Silvio Berlusconi's peccadilloes, liberal democracy remains intact. In some ways, the economic crisis is reclaiming the European Union for democracy from technocracy. The commission has opened itself up to extensive public consultations on all major new policies: these elicit strong levels of engagement, and their results are published in transparent fashion. Andrew Moravcsik has even suggested that "if the euro collapses it will be because of an abundance of democracy, as much as a lack of it." He holds that even after the crisis his seminal liberal-governmental framework still holds: that democratic input is adequately filtered through national governments in their negotiations at the EU level; that supranational competences are not great enough to make it necessary to "democratize the EU"; that welfare models are still determined purely by national variables; and that constitutional limits to majoritarian pluralism are a more apt measure of democracy than any spurious concern with participation.[57]

If predictions that democracy is under wholesale threat look overblown, the challenge to democracy is serious and responses to date have clearly not been adequate. Strengthening the ability of national parliaments to control decisions may be credible, but it is predicated on the assumption that all legitimacy flows through the pursuit of distinctive national interests and not any concept of a common European good. The intergovernmental model today looks far too relaxed and sanguine about the degree of democratic disconnect felt by besieged citizens. In turn, the European Parliament's role is unclear, as the new economic deals devised to address the crisis sit outside the EU institutions. Nor is it entirely clear whether a directly elected commission president would do much to relegitimize the EU, given that an election would not obviously inject a degree of clear policy choice to the body's largely technocratic functions. The problems with democracy run far too deep for any of these competing institutional fixes to make more than a modest dent. Rebooting European democracy can be achieved by neither purely national scrutiny over the EU nor a few additional federalized European Parliament powers. Rather, it must flow from a more qualitative reimagining—of a type that member states seem reluctant to engage in over five years into the crisis.

POWER SHIFTS: GERMAN HEGEMONY?

Another legacy of the crisis is a shift in political power and alliance structures. The postcrisis EU appears different in a crucial sense: Germany is unquestionably more dominant. Charles Grant quickly observed that Germany for the first time was now the uncontested leader in Europe, a fundamental change in the continent's political dynamics.[58] The much-repeated maxim is that the EU has been based on European states pretending not to notice Germany's rising power, in return for German commitments not to use that power in a heavy-handed way. The crisis appears to rupture that unspoken bargain. Monetary union was created to restrain Germany; its irony is that Germany is now more dominant than ever. Many politicians and observers worry that the facade of technocratic recipes for fiscal adjustments masks a fundamental shift in power among member states.

Ulrich Beck foresees a new "German empire" on the horizon.[59] He has become increasingly strident in this view: Europe at last has its single telephone, he insists, "and it belongs to Angela Merkel"; the continent now labors under a clear and pernicious structure of "hierarchical dependency" based on the yoke of "German euro-nationalism."[60] George Soros has attacked Berlin with vehemence: Germany has, he charges, created a fundamental division by choosing to play the role of selfish rather than benign hegemon, comfortable in the way the crisis has actually benefited its own exports and financing costs.[61] One extensive report concurs that Germany's "disproportionate" power over European politics combines with its inclination to think in terms of protecting its narrow national robustness rather than the systemic good.[62] Some of the language used in off-the-record conversations with diplomats or in seminars hints revealingly at the level of other member states' discomfort: "Germany is imposing regime change inside Europe." "This is 1945, but with Germany having won." "Our big choice now is whether we balance against or bandwagon with Germany." "We need the U.S. to counterbalance Germany."

Germany's unique position cannot be disassociated from the broader institutional strains that now tear at the union's roots. Updating his seminal book on the euro, David Marsh argues that Germany today is forced to prioritize its economic objectives over its political objectives; at one time, Germany thought the two were mutually reinforcing. Now, however, the choice is European unity versus monetary stability-cum-prudence. A reduced eurozone is the only way of finding a middle way through the impasse: "The economics of the euro are too fragmented to allow it to survive in the form of its first decade, but the politics are too entrenched to permit it to die." The political ramification is German dominion over a reduced, northern European currency bloc.[63]

Some of the most respected and perceptive commentators worry that the crisis's most abiding legacy is the counteraction against this weightier German power projection. Philip Stephens suggests that relations among EU member states have in consequence "returned to Westphalia."[64] Loukas Tsoukalis notes that even as they negotiate emergency solutions, fragile-feeling member states are "throwing stones at each other in a glasshouse."[65] Timothy Garton Ash concurs that the euro's rescue has been "a triumph of fear, not of hope," as it leaves a patina of anti-German bitterness across the continent.[66]

Yet, many observers suggest that German dominance for the moment remains heavily circumscribed. Some German analysts argue that much of the chatter about the extent of German power is nothing more than overblown scaremongering. Germany does not have the political will to become Europe's hegemon. Beyond its insistence on fiscal austerity, its lack of leadership is conspicuous.[67] This recalls Günter Grass's famous chronicle of Germany's slide into a becalmed, power-shirking, domesticated materialism after a century of ideological extremes.[68] Some German writers suggest that international leadership has never had less importance, support, or low profile in Germany.[69] One report rejects the notion that a new hierarchical balance of power has emerged, as Germany continues to resemble "a power without a purpose."[70] The most cited quip in recent years is the admission of Polish Foreign Minister Radosław Sikorski: "I fear German power less than I am beginning to fear German inactivity." Reflecting a common perception, one northern member state ambassador observes that Germany has "no idea what it wants strategically." Even the UK defense secretary laments that Germany is not playing enough of a lead role on defense and security matters.[71]

Some experts argue that Germany is in fact weaker as it has lost alliances. Debtor states have called its bluff to the extent that it cannot exit the euro without incurring even greater costs.[72] François Hollande's victory was interpreted primarily as an opportunity to tip alliances against Germany. The French president has made an overt effort to build alliances with other member states, distinct from the strategy of his predecessor, Nicolas Sarkozy, of sticking close to Germany against others. Consequently, it is France that is now seen as the center of a hub of shifting coalitions, evoking the bygone spirit of diplomatic master Talleyrand. Pairings of such countries as Spain and Poland, for example, are tightening relations in an effort to offset German power. Member states increasingly engage in "soft balancing" against Germany.

Germany has become increasingly nervous about pushing any long-term vision for Europe, fearing sensitivity from other member states to any templates coming out of Berlin. In 2013, Angela Merkel made a concerted effort to reach out to British Prime Minister David Cameron precisely to assuage fears of German dominance: in an EU without Britain, the counterbalance on Germany's weight would clearly be even less.

German diplomats remain extremely reticent about assertive uses of German power and insist that the EU dimension is essential to their own international projection. In lively Bundestag debates, many politicians have expressed unease with a new bilateralism in German foreign policy and the willingness of Foreign Minister (until the September 2013 elections) Guido Westerwelle to "go it alone" to build separate alliances with rising powers that cut across the diplomacy of EU partners. The Merkel government has declined to develop any national security strategy or to influence positively any geostrategic thinking at the EU level—with any international pretensions kept firmly out of the autumn election campaign.[73] Some analysts also suggest that the core economic underpinnings of German power are not that solid, as the country has itself failed to improve its underlying competitiveness by moving up the value-chain and into the services sector—and that, indeed, its reaction to the crisis has even delayed such a change by prioritizing manufacturing exports to China so heavily.[74] In late 2013, a large group of Germany's foremost foreign policy experts observed that the country remains "a global player in waiting"—not only due to its well-known military caution but even in terms of its hesitancy to use economic instruments to defend an open liberal order.[75]

Most Germans insist they do not want hegemony, are keen to avoid causing offense, and are almost hyper-aware of the antipathy their leadership would cause in other states. The crisis may even have made Germany less assertive on external questions as it becomes more attentive to concerns from others that it might be throwing its heavier weight around. Of all EU member states, Germany is still the one whose de facto level of assertiveness is most out of sync with the level of its structural power.

The trend has been toward not so much unrestrained German preeminence as varied constellations of shifting alliances. The politics of the euro crisis has revolved much more around shifting alliances and flexible, informal clusters. The specters of varying scenarios haunt the margins of EU summit negotiations, including those conjuring up a Europe of two speeds, multiple speeds, variable geometry, core-versus-periphery, and concentric circles. Crucially, this matter extends well beyond the UK's much-analyzed, embryonic estrangement from Europe. The evolution of the crisis has brought various forms of variable geometry to the fore. In the early stages of the crisis, the so-called Frankfurt Group emerged as a dominant grouping. The "Euro plus" pact progressed with twenty-three member states, absent the UK, the Czech Republic, Hungary, and Sweden. Flexible constellations of leadership and non-divisive subgroupings may go with the grain of differentiated contributions to problem solving. This will entail an effort to deepen "network diplomacy" over formal supranationalism. The crucial, unresolved question is whether voluntary nonparticipation can be made to prevail over forced marginalization. In short, the future balance between German power and more imaginatively dispersed power is not yet clear.

CONCLUSION

The crisis has bequeathed an unformed disquiet that now haunts the European dream. Many fear that given the delays to a deeper centralization of formal sovereignty, dissolution beckons. Notwithstanding fissiparous trends, however, the core pillars of the EU's model of integration for the moment remain standing. Josef Joffe insists that the crisis reveals such deep differences that "muddling through" is now even more the only likely route ahead.[76] Debate has been less about a new Europe than about replaying the familiar competition between intergovernmentalism and supranationalism. There has been neither a great leap forward in integration nor a shattering disintegration; at most the EU has shifted slightly more toward intergovermentalism, flexible constellations of leadership, and a modest ascendency of German power. Institutionally embedded patterns of cooperation have not been rendered obsolete by the structural shock of crisis. The EU's Kantian pact is battered and more than a little frayed, but it would be an exaggeration to suggest that "paradise" has been supplanted by the bruising world of unrestrained "power."

Economic policy mixes more state regulation with efforts at fiscal discipline but has not yet shifted into qualitatively new terrain. There appears no obvious way to turn for the continent's economic philosophy: neoliberal deregulation has failed but comprehensive, EU-tailored statist models of economic development are absent. While many fear that the most acute manifestations of the crisis may return, the likely course is one of a constantly fraught path being hewn: slightly too much austerity for deficit states to feel comfortable and slightly too much financial transfer for surplus states to feel entirely at ease, but without enough discomfort for either group of states to be utterly unable to bear the costs. Some observers predict a long and tension-inducing struggle to implement structural reform and regain competitiveness.[77]

The EU's legitimacy has taken a knock, and the sense of democratic powerlessness is palpable. Its tempering is less a matter of institutional fixes to the crisis per se than of EU decisionmaking catching up with new forms of representation and interest articulation. The crisis is not primarily that of an institutional democratic deficit, but a turbocharging of the deeper problems with democracy's increasing banality. Democracy cannot immunize against economic crisis, but it must allow meaningful choices to be made in response to a crisis. Proposals for political union have envisioned a slotting into place of the final "democracy" piece of the EU jigsaw. But they conceptualize such democracy in an extremely sanitized fashion.

The feeling is widespread that the EU still requires a new social contract to underpin revisions in its economic policy. Pawel Swieboda offers a sophisticated take, that those thinking that the crisis will usher in a new golden age and those who predict "the end of the EU" both miss the central point: a qualitative change is needed, given that the "European contract" underpinning integration policies "is now broken and needs to be redesigned."[78] A vibrant political process has to be the prerequisite to nascent moves toward political union. If such a process is flattened or circumvented, the problems supposedly attacked may merely worsen. European governments are to be reproached for having done pitifully little since the beginning of the crisis to reconstitute the union's grand bargain, this time from the bottom up.

CHAPTER 3

BOON OR BANE FOR EUROPEAN GLOBAL INFLUENCE?

The dissection of the crisis's different internal dimensions lays the foundations for understanding its broader global consequences. Moving beyond the immediate crisis itself, it is possible to begin assessing how serious a dent this has left in the EU's global presence and influence. This external spillover has received relatively little attention. But the age of fragility reigns both internally and externally. In the period after 9/11, the primary focus was on the challenges coming at Europe from outside and the impact they had on domestic policies. Much better appreciation is now required of the reverse dynamics of internal-to-external linkages. This chapter maps the way in which the internal euro crisis has spilled over to condition the core determinants of foreign policy effectiveness. Such linkages remain a moving target, and the subject of speculation as tangible impacts only gradually reveal themselves. Yet it can be contended that varied trends are at work. Several reasons exist to expect a negative spillover to external policies, but also why a more positive impact might emerge. While the crisis has undoubtedly wreaked huge damage on the EU's global power and standing, this may at least be partially offset by more positive spillover dynamics that are afoot.

IMPOVERISHED POWER

The politics of debt have for many centuries conditioned power balances—from the rivalry of Italian city-states, the course of the Napoleonic Wars, the fate of empires, the twists of the American Civil War, right through to the frustrated transitions of the post–Cold War third wave of democratization.[1] And the eurozone crisis is no exception, leaving a material dent on the EU's global reach. Optimists stress that the EU's postcrisis share of global trade is still high and its military power is still comfortably in excess of that of rising powers; they also predict that the euro will retain its role as the world's second reserve currency. Yet many statistics suggest that in at least some ways the crisis has moderately accelerated the EU's incremental, relative decline.

Europe's global structural presence has diminished on several axes, although not by as much as might have been expected considering the depth of the crisis. The West-to-East power shift has certainly been put on turbo-boost simply by virtue of a core redistribution of resources: the gap has yawned wider between the surpluses held in developing economies and the debt mountain in parts of Europe. In terms of resource commitments to foreign policy, a biblical run of lean years threatens. The amounts of money spent internally to save the euro have exceeded many times over the resources available for external relations objectives.

Europe's commercial presence has lost ground, even if it has not dramatically collapsed across all indicators. The EU's share of global exports declined from 16.4 percent in 2007 to 14.7 percent in 2012; over the same period, its share of global imports decreased from 18.4 to 15.4 percent.[2] More seriously, outward FDI from EU states fell by over 50 percent in 2012; inward investment declined over 30 percent, to a level only one third of its 2008 level. A staggering 70 percent of the global reduction in foreign investment in 2012 was accounted for by this EU fall.[3] In 2012, developing states for the first time received more inward investment than developed states ($680 billion compared with $550 billion). The EU has remained the world's biggest exporter, and its global market share of commerce has not fallen as much as those of the United States or Japan over the past decade. But EU trade flows have increased at a far slower rate than those of other powers. Guido Westerwelle acknowledged that the bottom-line impact of the crisis is that the EU's economic performance is now more dependent on rising powers than the latter are on Europe's growth.[4]

By the end of the crisis, the EU will certainly have ceded much potential in global currency matters. The euro's share of foreign reserve holdings increased from 19 percent in 2001 to 28 percent by 2009; by 2013 it had fallen back to 23 percent. Rising powers had been keen to see a further rise of the euro, which would facilitate their diversification out of dollars. The ECB reined this enthusiasm back for fear that EU deficits were too small to fund a huge uptake of euros globally, a move that in particular left China disillusioned. Now there is more focus on the renminbi being the future challenger to dollar supremacy. Commissioners still stress that the euro will remain the world's second reserve currency and that it will be used just as widely as before the crisis. And, indeed, Russia and some Gulf states, among others, have increased their euro holdings. The fear of a smaller eurozone robbing the EU of much of its monetary weight has, of course, not come to pass, at least so far. Yet, the euro's share of foreign reserve holdings has now been declining for four years.

The amount of EU debt held by entities outside Europe has increased significantly. The relative clout of the European banking sector has been reduced on a global level. Banks' margin of financial maneuvering to act beyond the EU has diminished; the priority is financing the internal market. By 2012, more than 90 percent of IMF commitments were in European states. The uncertainties of the crisis pushed Asian surplus countries to hold more, not fewer, resources, exacerbating imbalances; higher interest rates associated with stringency rewarded them for increasing their surpluses.[5] Pressure on banks to lend locally and increased liquidity requirements have led to the retraction of European capital from around the world—diluting economic influence. According to the Institute of International Finance, the EU's crisis was the main cause of a sizable reduction in net private capital flows to emerging markets between 2010 and 2012.[6] European governments even had to beg Russia to help with the bailout for Cyprus. Indeed, in contrast to most European states' fortunes, Russian foreign exchange reserves have increased since the beginning of the financial crisis in 2008 to be the third-largest holdings in the world. The bumpy road to fuller monetary integration risks financially exhausting member states and constricting their ambitions in global currency diplomacy.

More direct measures of external capacity have also followed a negative trend. European governments have dramatically reduced military expenditure. Major defense cuts have been slated for the period up to 2014–2015. Beginning in 2012, Germany planned to reduce its defense budget by 25 percent; the UK by 7.5 percent; Spain by 7 percent; Ireland by 15 percent; Austria by 20 percent; Belgium by 10 percent; and some central and eastern European states by up to 50 percent. These were minimum reductions, with most governments indicating that the cutbacks were likely to deepen to yet unspecified levels. Italy made a particularly sizable cut in 2012 of more than 10 percent. The Netherlands also planned an unprecedented scaling back, for example, whittling down the size of a controversial order for new fighter aircraft. Significantly, there has been little coordination in the cutbacks, meaning that member states have cut on similar capabilities rather than specializing on different items. Two notable exceptions have been Poland and, ironically, Denmark, which opted out of the EU's Common Security and Defense Policy; both have slightly increased defense spending—Poland by 7 percent in 2012.[7] Estonia has also recovered from a deep economic downturn to raise its defense spending to 2 percent of GDP in 2013.

Meanwhile, rising powers have increased their defense capabilities significantly. Since 2010, the EU is the only region where defense spending has declined. Five emerging powers (Brazil, Russia, India, and China—known as the BRICs—plus Saudi Arabia) are now among the top ten defense spenders globally. Asia overtook Europe in defense expenditure in 2012.[8]

In an April 2013 white paper, the French government announced that its core defense expenditure would be maintained at roughly the same level for three years but that military personnel would be cut by 10 percent and rapid deployment capacity by nearly 50 percent, with broader reductions in overall spending to follow up to 2020. In July 2012 it was announced that British army personnel were to be reduced by 20 percent, to the lowest level since the Napoleonic Wars. An even deeper round of cuts was announced at the end of 2012. In 2012, the Spanish government cut back 20,000 troops and announced a further 15,000 reduction in the pipeline. Much equipment has been rendered inoperable as repair bills can simply not be met. Taken together, these defense cuts will leave Europe even further behind in the most advanced technological and qualitative improvements in capability in a way that will not be easy to recover even if budgets increase as the crisis recedes.

Development budgets have also suffered, although some European donors have retained a laudable level of commitment to poverty reduction in the developing world throughout the recession. Overall EU development aid (Commission plus member state allocations) decreased in 2011 for the first time in fifteen years, by just over 6 percent. It then fell a further 2 billion euros in 2012.[9] The biggest cuts came from Spain and Greece; Germany and Sweden were the two states that still slightly increased development assistance.[10] UK aid fell by only 0.6 percent between 2011 and 2012; at 8.9 billion pounds, it was still the second-highest annual amount ever and 50 percent above the amount in 2008 when the crisis began. Dutch aid decreased in 2011–2012 by just under 2 billion euros, from 0.8 to 0.7 percent of GDP, and the number of country recipients of this aid from 33 to 15. Spanish development assistance was cut by more than 70 percent after 2011. Spain closed embassies in Yemen and Zimbabwe, and in 2012 the Foreign Ministry's budget was cut in half. Member states rejected the Commission's bid for increased funds for the European Neighborhood Policy in the 2014–2020 budget, refusing to authorize any real-term expansion in aid for this period.

More than $7 trillion was spent on bailouts, yet far more modest foreign policy budgets have been shorn back. Nongovernmental organizations (NGOs) have strongly criticized the cuts as disproportionate, in that development budgets have been cut by more than GDP reductions.[11] In 2013 Turkey is set to overtake Spain as an aid donor. India now gives $1.5 billion in development aid, on par with all except the big European donors.

Many diplomats and analysts have expressed concern that the impact of the crisis on EU structural presence has bred a gnawing insularity. In conversation, policymakers routinely suggest that the precariousness of the whole EU integration project means that external policies will be accorded a lower priority for the foreseeable future. This has been a theme of postcrisis debates in the European Parliament, with politicians criticizing foreign ministers' subjugation to finance ministers and central bank officials. One policy planner summarizes the prevailing view succinctly: "Foreign policy is a secondary question now." One of the External Action Service's most respected and thoughtful managers laments that efforts to devise a comprehensive geostrategic assessment of the crisis have failed to bear fruit. A general view pervades Brussels that heightened ambition for foreign policy awaits the arrival of a new team of Commissioners and High Representative in 2014. On the back of such developments, the EU looks set to be an increasingly muted power.

POWER AFTER ATTRACTION?

If the EU's global influence has flowed in part from the example of its own integration experience, the mismanagement of the current crisis has left a sizable dent in this form of appeal. Global, or external, influence can no longer be assumed to follow smoothly from the successes of internal integration. When democracy is being hollowed of de facto meaning within many European states, many ask whether the EU can still, with the same degree of legitimacy, urge better quality accountability and democracy on other states. Richard Gowan detects that the EU's strictures to the world on effective multilateralism now lack credibility when interstate cooperation within Europe has been so rocky during the crisis.[12] The 2012 European Council on Foreign Relations Scorecard opines dramatically that the EU's global image has suffered a "role reversal from solution to a problem … [from] being a subject to being an object." It asserts that the value of Europe as an ideal has been roundly degraded.[13] Even if this judgment may be unduly harsh, interviewees certainly worry that the EU is losing credibility as a distinctive form of governance, since the solutions being touted seem to replicate the pathologies and inadequacies of the nation-state. Descending from inspiration to ignominy, the union is a murkier light to the world.

One senior EAS diplomat acknowledges the challenge of better understanding the more "indirect spillover" from the crisis: beyond the budget cuts for external relations are the issues of declining support for enlargement of the union and weakening soft power. The more candid EU officials recognize that the union needs to move from an ingrained narrative that "Europe is the solution" to accepting that—even if it might be exaggerated to say "Europe is the problem"—its standing in international affairs is now more mixed. In practice it is proving difficult for the EU to make this switch. Aggressive and even coercive externalization of the EU's own internal market rules—"market power Europe"—is still seen as the basis of the union's sway over others and an unerring fillip to pro-liberal market multilateralism.[14] One EU research project concludes that the future is one of regional hubs setting rules in their own immediate spheres, with global organizations fading away; within this scenario the EU's influence will still be that of rule-setter for its neighborhood.[15] Yet such traditionally cast lenses are now more widely questioned. Some academics have, for example, assembled data that more critically question the long-standing and central assumption that greater unity among member states will automatically translate into more effective European power.[16]

The waning of the EU's power-by-attraction can be witnessed at different levels. One level relates to matters of global financial regulation. The appeal of EU financial standards and models has weakened. The complexities of the ad hoc and myriad integrative commitments taken to resolve the crisis have in some senses rendered the EU model even more one of a kind and removed from the regulatory experiences of other powers. Before the crisis, the EU was widely defined as a superpower in the realm of international financial standards, with only the United States of comparable weight. Since the crisis, however, the picture is different. Finance is now more politicized: technocrats are under greater domestic constraints, which tilts the focus away from internationally disseminated standards and back toward home country control. While this does not signal the end of international standards, it does mean that these will set broader norms now, be based more around mutual recognition, and leave more room for national variation.[17] The broader result of the crisis is a wider spread in the varieties of capitalism across the world, and less emulation of EU models. At a fateful G20 meeting in Los Cabos in 2012, the rest of the world ganged up to question the EU's ability to make basic decisions to avert contagious financial meltdown. The union's regulatory governance was suddenly the subject of more ire than awe.

Another level of diminished sway pertains to the EU's relations with rising powers. In the wake of the crisis, the dynamics of the EU's relations with many emerging powers have altered. These relations were once seen as a matter of how much of the EU's "way of doing things" the partner country was willing and able to take on board. Now, while other powers certainly still seek to learn from the European experience, they approach the EU at least in part as a strategic challenge to be managed. Turks even joke that today EU membership might entail having to bail out Greece. The turnaround is seen in the evolution of the EU's formalized strategic partnerships, the policy mechanism devised to channel relations with key powers. Giovanni Grevi argues that because of the crisis, these partnerships have become primarily about the EU reassuring itself of its own worth; the EU no longer mainly supplies political recognition but increasingly seeks such recognition.[18]

Since signing its strategic partnership with the EU in 2007, Brazil has actually been more assertively confrontational with EU regulatory and foreign policy positions. In late 2011, Brazil coordinated with other BRICs over possible action toward the euro crisis rather than directly with the EU on a bilateral basis—clearly treating the EU more as a problem than a partner. The then Brazilian foreign minister taunted: "Note that it was not Brazil who proposed a strategic partnership with the EU. The proposal came from them." The EU was portrayed as the cap-in-hand, inferior member of the partnership.[19] The EU signed a strategic partnership with Mexico because of the country's close relationship with the United States and concerns over drug trafficking, but it later palpably lost influence and failed to fashion any kind of strategic coordination. The most frequent—and least surprising—comment from diplomats of all such medium powers is that the crisis has undermined the EU's appeal as the shining model of regional cooperation. An ambassador for one rising power opines more generally: "For us, the EU is no longer the global magnet."

At another level of influence, in the Balkans and Eastern neighborhood, the gravitational pull of the EU model has not entirely dissipated. But it is struggling to retain the same degree of hold. In the Balkans, EU agreements are inching forward; this is clearly a region where the EU has retained some magnetic pull. Catherine Ashton mediated a deal between Serbia and Kosovo in May 2013 that may in time revive Serbia's relations with the EU. Yet, as the prospect of further enlargement seems increasingly remote, the EU has also struggled to ward off resurgent instability in the region, in particular in Bosnia. Some Balkan states are once again flirting with Russia. Turkish influence now cuts across the EU, too. European transformative power is more circumscribed, with the region suspended in a kind of partial inclusion. Serbian negotiators report that the euro crisis has "definitely delayed" accession.[20] Some countries of the Eastern Partnership—Ukraine, Georgia, and Moldova—still proclaim a strong European orientation but have expressed disappointment with the union, as they look apprehensively to Russia's more direct influence over the region. Armenia, Azerbaijan, and Belarus have become more resistant to EU influence than they were several years ago. In summer 2013 Armenia made the shock decision to join the Russian-led Eurasian customs union rather than sign a new EU association agreement. As this book went to press, the Ukrainian government caused an even greater stir by pulling out of its association agreement, after pressure from Russia—although it claimed still to be committed to a European orientation.

Finally, while not easy to quantify, the spillover between Europe's internal democratic travails and the credibility of external policies should not be underestimated. The challenges to democracy within the union are not without importance for the EU's global, normative legitimacy. Postcrisis, the internal and external can no longer be conceptually held separate.[21] At a policy level, the internal-external linkage has received little attention: global action is still seen as a residual, not integral for pro-democratic internal developments.[22] The ill-health of the West's own democracy weakens the domestic foundations of the EU's normative influence around the world.

DISUNITED ON THE GLOBAL STAGE

The fundamental divide over economic policy has spread like an infection into the EU's external image. This is where a spillover is evidence of the power realignment and fragmentation outlined in chapter two; it is a core sense in which the features of the internal crisis have had a causal impact on external policies. Many analysts, journalists, and policymakers have observed a general ethos of schism and discord within the EU's foreign policy machinery.

At a most visceral level, the crisis has dented the European "we-feeling" requisite to an effectively united set of external policies. Internal economic divergence has engendered variation in member states' foreign policy visions. In the most direct sense, internal economic differences have precluded convergence of governments' external plans. The much-cited 2003 Habermas-Derrida proclamation that a European identity had been born around a foreign policy diametrically opposed to that of the United States rubs uneasily with reality a decade on.[23] In 1997 Martin Feldstein predicted that the euro would cause such strains economically that it would also usher in tensions among member states across a whole range of other issues.[24] Although no dramatic falling-out has occurred in practice, the crisis has left both surplus and deficit governments feeling that a self-help prioritization of national interests is often preferable to complicated efforts at EU foreign policy coordination. With both debtor and creditor countries perceiving themselves to be victims of the crisis, their store of goodwill toward foreign policy coordination seems depleted. The pressure is toward surplus states concluding that the core EU could recover international influence only by ditching weaker, deficit countries.[25] Charles Kupchan sees the crisis as a symptom of the "renationalization of European politics" that has distanced the EU even further from "the collective governance that Europe needs to thrive in a globalized world."[26]

Compounding such policy calculations, global markets are less convinced than before the crisis that the EU should rightfully be seen as a single bloc in international matters. Jean Pisani-Ferry observes that international markets have begun to treat the different parts of the European Union economy as separate blocs, portending a broader fragmentation across the gamut of policy sectors.[27] Differentiated commitments as regards the euro and attendant rescue packages have engendered contrasting external preferences. As an extension of a divide between a core and outer Europe, members of the core have begun caucusing on a broader range of external policy issues. This applies in particular to issues of global financial governance that touch upon fiscal and other financial questions.

The *Economist* perceived a very direct and negative impact: in the sphere of international policy, the euro crisis has given birth to a "two-belief" Europe, with an inward-looking core fundamentally at odds with an outward-looking, liberal periphery.[28] Others insist that the purely economic-technocratic tenor of euro crisis management has left the EU bereft of common ideational elements capable of tying member states more resolutely together on the international stage. From this perspective, the political dimensions of the internal crisis pose an equally political challenge for EU global policy.[29] Joschka Fischer believes that postcrisis EU foreign policy suffers from creeping "renationalization" and "provincialism."[30]

Paradoxically, the Lisbon Treaty seems to have produced a shift in the center of gravity of foreign policymaking back to national capitals and hence more defensive reneging on unity commitments. The gap between formal, unity-enticing rules and practice is widening. The EU has declined to update the European Security Strategy because postcrisis strategic visions resist convergence. British officials report that the Conservative-led government quite clearly now believes that security and defense interests can be delinked from the fate of the EU as such and that the key aim is to retain more practical, bilateral cooperation with France. Conversely, more than one diplomat is wont to speculate that the French government has been positively enthusiastic about using the crisis to eject the UK from the heart of EU foreign policy. One former insider notes that member states now "tend to formulate national positions without coordinating with their partners."[31] The Big Three—the UK, Germany, and France—have perceived greater room for national maneuver in a world of middle powers and shifting alliances around the world.[32] Crisis has brought to the surface a much longer trend of Germany reassessing its national interests and a "power politics re-socialization" and "de-Europeanization" of German foreign policy.[33] Angela Merkel's veto of the putative merger between BAE Systems and EADS at the end of 2012 undermined hopes for a cooperative, European-level defense company.

The rest of the world now perceives there to be far bigger divisions among member states; other states might judge these divisions to be bigger than they really are, but that in itself constitutes a challenge to EU commonality. The perception is strong in rising powers that the crisis has widened cracks between member states and thus that they need to engage more at the national level to safeguard their varied interests.

While Greece may take much blame for disastrous economic management, other EU states could be upbraided for having failed to think through the broader geopolitical and foreign policy consequences of their economic strictures: a Greece that returns to a more hostile form of nationalism toward Turkey; closes itself against enlargement to the Balkans; withdraws from active engagement with Israel and with Arab partners; plays politics with the various pipelines set to cross Greek territory; and reverts to a more pro-Russian strategic outlook.[34] Diplomats worry that Greece's weaknesses will make Athens an even less dependable foreign policy partner.

More broadly than the crisis per se, some realist writers see structural changes at work that could potentially cause fissures in the union. They interpret the euro crisis as the manifestation of broader underlying global political dynamics: in the multipolar world, there is no single, overwhelmingly threatening power against which the EU needs to "balance," removing the main driving force for integration and gradually weakening the glue binding member states together in the most general strategic sense.[35] A multipolar global order may be engendering competitive multipolarity within Europe, too. The EU has traditionally been seen as an incipient subsystem of the emerging system of global governance. But the rise of the BRICs has had the effect of encouraging member states to seek international influence through various levels of agency, resulting in a fracturing of the EU's role as the central pillar holding up a liberal form of global governance.[36]

SILVER-LINED ADVERSITY?

Much in these dispiriting critiques is incontrovertible. At myriad levels the crisis has presented a sobering and acute challenge for European foreign policy. Internal crisis has indeed left its mark on external power, vibrancy, and unity. However, the pressures have not run in only one direction. Countering such gloomy trends, some writers have detected a more positive spillover from the crisis to external policies. And evidence for this line of reasoning is not entirely absent. In at least some modest regard, the crisis may have exerted a positive impact on the EU's external influence, agility, and unity.

Crisis can be understood as implosion or as stimulant. Luuk van Middelaar, Herman Van Rompuy's speechwriter, makes a seminal point in his erudite analysis of European integration: the key feature of the continent's political history has been an ability to update its model of cooperation in response to crisis. Looked at in terms of such a larger sweep, the current crisis is not so much a qualitatively distinctive event but part of this same recurrent testing of "the Union's extraordinary capacity to metamorphose under the pressure of events ... to absorb a shock and come out profoundly renewed." Van Middelaar contends that "not since 1945 have [European] populations been so conscious of sharing a common destiny."[37]

Following this line of hopeful reasoning, five reasons for optimism are evident:

Integration logic. First, a step forward in economic integration may begin to generate dynamics that encourage a spillover to deeper foreign policy cooperation. Prominent academics detect a broad resuscitation of so-called neo-functionalist dynamics, with the crisis pushing the "integration frontier" forward across a whole range of issues.[38] Richard Rosecrance believes that deeper economic union will provide the overdue fillip to the EU's external power and finally allow it to take on Asia's rising powers.[39] Many voices express confidence that the crisis represents more of an opportunity than a catastrophe and that the EU is set to emerge strengthened. A common refrain is that the EU has on many occasions been propelled forward by the focusing effect of a crisis. José Manuel Barroso has insisted that the "crisis has forced Europe to rethink our economic model. The Europe that emerges from this crisis will be a Europe more fit for this new interdependent world."[40]

Some observers insist that it is impossible to have political union while the EU's Common Foreign and Security Policy remains intergovernmental and with separate national foreign policies. Proposals for political union have included plans for a fully supranational foreign and security policy. The report produced by eleven foreign ministers in September 2012 marked a notable attempt to map out a vision for a more integrated Common Foreign and Security Policy, along with a European army. The report was not officially taken up, but its presentation was in itself significant. At the end of 2012, France, Germany, Italy, Poland, and Spain agreed to support a new "military structure" to oversee common European conflict resolution missions.

Spillover in the defense sphere has advanced even further in 2013. The December 2012 EU summit charged the European Commission and the European External Action Service with drawing up proposals to strengthen the EU's security policy and defense capabilities. Leaders committed to discussing defense cooperation at a summit in December 2013, for the first time since 2008. Senior diplomats opined that this was the clearest case of the eurozone crisis pushing governments to cooperate: the summit was billed as an opportunity to send the message that the EU would remain a serious security player. An interim report in preparation for the council published in July 2013 demonstrated a high level of ambition to make CSDP supportive of a broader postcrisis EU foreign policy recalibration and not just about small-scale training initiatives in crisis zones.[41]

While day-to-day decisionmaking has strained unity, ministers have at least formally recognized that the crisis invites a commitment to deepening foreign policy coordination. Governments have promised stronger unity on many occasions, repeatedly making the point that discord in foreign policy would be untenable in a more integrated economic union. Of course, such promises of unity rub against the reality of the measures those same governments have adopted in practice. But it is not without meaning that at least in formal terms, the crisis has given a new lease on life to cooperative commitments.

Structural logic. Second, the crisis actually strengthens the structural reasons for unity. It may be that such structural imperatives of global competition will temper the scenario of a "two-belief" Europe. Member states will need to unite around an effective form of global commercial policy. Their differences on internal fiscal policies need not prevent consensus taking shape on such an external policy; indeed, they do not weigh against the external, structural reasons that should encourage all member states to be in accord on foreign policy. The binding effect of the global economy's structural parameters might be expected at least partially to offset any centrifugal impact of member states' short-term crisis management. Citing precisely these imperatives, the Italian, Swedish, Spanish, and Polish governments kick-started a process aimed at a European Global Strategy—a proposal for which was presented in the autumn of 2013.[42]

Many academics reject the realist argument that, with the demise of the Soviet Union and now weakening of the United States, the EU lacks a structural rationale to bind its member states together. They insist that the habits of cooperation and shared problem solving in foreign policy have progressed too far to be easily reversible and, crucially, that the reshaped world order requires the kind of pragmatic joint management of new challenges that will bring EU governments closer together. Thus, there is both a remolded, exogenous, or structural realist motive for deeper coordination and an internal self-sustaining momentum to deeper foreign policy convergence.[43] Some have made the argument categorically: fifty years of socialization and an embedded "security community" ensures that a shrinking of the eurozone would not take Europe back to the division and aggressive nationalism of the prewar period.[44] Even if the crisis weakens certain EU institutional structures, it is unlikely to unravel the deeper roots of this European "security community" because peace is ensured though deep interdependence, shared values, and the cement of other institutions such as NATO.[45]

A more prosaic part of this binding force derives from a cost-saving logic. The need to avoid expensive duplication has become acknowledged as more pressing because of the crisis. Spain has moved toward double-hatting its diplomats in some EU delegations. Military asset sharing has moved into a higher gear. In February 2012 the UK and France signed another agreement to deepen defense cooperation, through an integrated maritime fleet, joint exercises in the Mediterranean, and inception of a joint expeditionary force by 2016. Germany and Italy have also signed a memorandum on procurement cooperation. Smaller groupings of Nordic states, the Benelux group (Belgium, the Netherlands, and Luxembourg), and the Visegrad group (the Czech Republic, Hungary, Poland, and Slovakia) have similarly deepened such cooperation. The 2010 Ghent framework has given a coordinating umbrella for these various pooling and sharing initiatives. NATO's Smart Defense initiative has taken the trend further. In 2012 the European Defense Agency was given a strengthened statute, and the defense sector was opened to more single market discipline in 2009.[46] At the end of 2012, member states agreed on a new Code of Conduct for Pooling and Sharing. A European Commission Task Force on Defense Industries and Markets has explored ways of removing barriers to cooperation among defense firms. The December 2013 defense summit was set to be primarily about firming up such cost-sharing commitments. The NATO secretary general said the summit was "an opportunity not to be missed," and threw his weight behind the Commission proposals for a Europeanized modernization of capabilities. He argued in September 2013 that if this were not achieved then defense cuts could reach the point where in the future most member states would not be equipped to participate in crisis management operations to any meaningful degree.[47]

Senior officials say they have been inundated with calls from member states pressing the EAS to assume a lead on foreign policy because national governments are constrained by the recession. One ambassador insists that member states' preoccupation with the economic crisis has been an opportunity for allowing the EAS more space to craft a common strategic vision. Catherine Ashton has begun to find niche areas of leadership in the midst of the crisis, on Iran, Kosovo, and human rights, for example. This reflects a familiar logic of the two-level game, with member states, for their own crisis-linked reasons, actually wanting to hand more foreign policy responsibility to the EU level. There has been some deepening of what Anand Menon skillfully referred to as the union's "paradox of politics": national governments have ironically availed themselves of greater maneuverability often by passing the buck for difficult foreign relations issues to the EU level.[48]

Compensation logic. Third, a logic of compensation may be detected. Because the crisis has undermined the internal credibility of the EU, some far-sighted diplomats and ministers have recognized that a focus on values in foreign policy has become more essential as a legitimizing logic of a new EU narrative. UK officials claim to see at least some need to deepen cooperation on foreign policy in order to compensate partially for their marginalization from the core economic union. Similarly, Germany and France have looked for areas to keep the UK from drifting too far apart; foreign and security policy is the most obvious possibility. The UK and France cannot afford to fall out over foreign policy because they are poles apart on economic policy; Germany and France do fall out on foreign policy because they are so committed to cooperating on the economic crisis. The Franco-British defense accord was made explicitly to offset disagreements over the euro. Part of the UK-France deal is to cooperate on nuclear technology exports, diametrically opposed to the German decision to phase out nuclear power. EAS officials have spun a sophisticated narrative that the crisis not only makes a stronger case for unity and the avoidance of duplication across all areas of external relations, but also requires success stories of how the EU's Common Security and Defense Policy (CSDP) helps trade, as in the case of the Atalanta mission policing sea-lanes off the Horn of Africa. Three new CSDP missions deployed in 2012: to enhance maritime capacity around the Horn of Africa; to protect an airport in South Sudan; and to train security services in Niger. The EU launched a new defense cooperation dialogue with Brazil in 2012. Plans for a European Institute for Peace are progressing.

Flexibility logic. Fourth, a slightly different argument is that at least some aspects of flexibility may boost external effectiveness. Some observers predict a complex series of varying constellations of member states leading cooperation in different policy areas. The UK may be opposed to fiscal cooperation but can remain a leader in foreign policy, on which Germany may remain lukewarm. One insider insists this can be more beneficial in overall terms to foreign and security policy.[49] The former head of the European Council's legal service argues that only a two-speed Europe can return strength and flexibility to the EU and its global image.[50] The notion of flexible integration could be seen as fitting well with the global trend in regionalization: more flexible and open forms of cooperation built around interregional linkages of pivotal regional powers. Dominique Moïsi suggests that flexible combinations of national and European measures may have the positive side effect of mobilizing populations to compete more effectively against Asian and other powers.[51] Greece has long blocked so many foreign policy decisions; some suggest that these barriers will be more easily circumvented after the crisis.

In particular, enlargement may become more feasible in a modified form. A more loosely integrated "outer ring" of EU membership may help dissipate tensions over enlargement. While some elaborate institutional engineering would be required, candidates for membership may more readily be welcomed into a formalized outer grouping made up of states that are more favorable to enlargement than France or Germany—although it is not clear how attractive an option this would be for such aspirants. Flexible integration could be marshaled as a useful foreign policy instrument. There may be more positive potential as the standard enlargement model appears to have run aground, and export of the maximum possible acquis (or formal union rules) also to eastern and southern noncandidates is now a more questionable basis for the EU's neighborhood policy. Graduated membership is becoming a seriously debated option among candidates and aspirants frustrated at years of EU procrastination and delay. Some suggest it could be an attractive option if outsiders could choose their level of membership and were able to "join" full EU meetings at least in those sectors where detailed negotiations had been concluded. One former Turkish minister opines that a more flexible EU would represent a "fantastic opportunity" for Turkey. The crisis has combined with a reemergence of the "British problem" to engender new consideration of an "Economic Area–plus." This could be used not only for the UK but also to incorporate Turkey and other potential applicant states into an arrangement in which (unlike the current

European Economic Area) outer core states would have a formal say over those areas in which they participate.

Adaptive logic. Fifth, some commentators insist that the crisis has actually enhanced the EU's power of attraction and appeal. They maintain that the EU's management of the crisis boosts its "influence by example." The EU can actually win more global appeal as a space for managing difference and as a governance laboratory rather than through the export of fixed rules and standards. Many academic cheerleaders of the EU's form of global action have stuck to their guns: other powers are engaging in "open international aggression" against Europe to take advantage of the EU's undeserved travails; the crisis will confirm and deepen the EU's commitment to innovative political integration; and its successful joint management of the crisis will stand as a model for effective multilateralism to other regions, actually more effective "as an answer to unregulated globalization and market diktats."[52] Even as the crisis deepened, such analysts insisted that EU influence was on the rise, that its appeal to others as a model of pooled governance continued to grow, as a Weberian ideal–type management of globalization, a source of spontaneous emulation and as a "collective power" not limited to acting on its own interests but on those of all humankind.[53] Some experts insist that the crisis has prompted the EU to engage in the kind of flexible, multilevel problem solving that will make it more able to prosper in the new world order.[54] Counterintuitively, Gulf states have recently shown more of an interest in the EU as offering useful lessons for their own putative Gulf Union.

One prevalent view is that the euro crisis is best understood as but one manifestation of a crisis of globalization. A degree of deglobalization is possible as markets and democracy clash so resoundingly—a reckoning long foretold. And the EU has been in the eye of the storm simply because it is ahead of the curve in facing up to this inevitable clashing of economics and politics. Pawel Swieboda points out: "The eurozone crisis is a microcosm of what is happening at the global level" in terms of fundamental cleavages between deficit and surplus countries, and the solution requires not only redesign within the EU but also a more balanced global monetary system.[55] Some observers believe that the EU's attraction has strengthened as it is seen as dealing effectively with problems that also beset the wider global economy. Harold James puts this point of view well: "The current crisis involves two sets of problems—one is genuinely global, and not particularly European; the other is peculiar to the problem of monetary union without a corresponding state." He intimates that, if part of the crisis is a global one—fiscal overstretch and imbalances—the EU's strenuous efforts at crisis management might turn out to reflect not so much a weakness but leadership in providing solutions applicable to the broader international system.[56]

CONCLUSION

Walter Laqueur caused much controversy in predicting the "end of Europe" well before the crisis; he remains doubtful whether the "deep crisis awakens [the EU] from its slumber" and if Europe "realises it is facing a crisis of survival."[57] The economic crisis has indeed shaken the foundations upon which efforts to construct a united and effective EU foreign policy rest. The indicators of relative, structural decline have accelerated. The shine on the EU's global image is less glistening. While the need for deeper unity and engagement seems clear in the postcrisis world, in practice member states seem further apart on many of the big geostrategic questions than before the crisis. Europe's crisis has pushed strategic primacy back to national capitals in a way that may provide for beneficial short-term flexibility but that augurs badly for the longer term if not kept within manageable parameters. The financial crisis is undoubtedly a serious constraint, and future core-periphery institutional change is now uncertain. It is of serious concern that this has not encouraged member states to work together to temper strategic shrinkage. From a large number of senior policymakers, this author has heard the same refrain over and over: there is no vision of where the EU should be globally in the medium term, beyond desperately defending what currently exists within Europe as the euro crisis tightens its grip.

However, notwithstanding the worrying spillover effects of the domestic euro crisis and the ubiquitous warnings that internal fracture will fatally undermine EU foreign policy unity, the centrifugal effect of the economic crisis on external policy still needs to be fully monitored as trends unfold in multiple directions. Suggestive of the more subtle impact on the way that European influence manifests itself, it is striking that defense cuts have not been debated in terms of an existential risk to national security in the way that they have been debated in the United States.[58] A middle course can be staked out between utter Euro-condemnation, on the one hand, and the Panglossian insistence that crisis merely reaffirms the EU's innovative advantages, on the other hand. The "crisis as opportunity" line may appear to be astoundingly immodest and insensitive to those who have suffered as a result of the sheer magnitude of recession and financial mismanagement. And the list of the crisis's potentially positive benefits certainly contains much that is little more than loosely grounded wishful thinking—that the specter of Hegel's cunning of reason can somehow be conjured into the Brussels hallways. But there is merit in trying to see through the fog of short-term restraints. Recall that mythological Europa becomes a unifier after the tragedy of her abduction. While recent economic and structural factors have combined to leave their indelible mark, governments' strategic choices can still influence the balance between negative and positive international spillovers from the euro crisis.

CHAPTER 4

GEOECONOMIC EUROPE

The economic crisis has rendered more prominent the geoeconomic dimension of international power and presence. Effective geoeconomic strategies are crucial to European recovery. This chimes with the widely made observation that geoeconomics—defined as states' strategic deployment of resources to advance economic interests—is also a more central underpinning of the emerging post-Western world order. The world is becoming more geoeconomic. International trends are increasingly conditioned by the use of statecraft for economic ends; a focus on relative economic gain and power; a concern with gaining control of resources; the enmeshing of state and business sectors; and the primacy of economic over other forms of security.[1] In the field of trade and commerce, the pincer of internal and external constraints has become a clearly evident shaper of EU strategy.

In response to the crisis, the EU and its member states have become notably more geoeconomic in their international outlook. In this regard, a spillover from pressures on the EU's domestic economic model—outlined in chapter two—has affected external economic policy. Internal austerity has increased the need for external trade promotion. The EU has justifiably seen the need to be more effective in the pursuit of its global economic interests as it battles its difficult financial straits. Geoeconomic thinking is an increasingly important shaper of EU external policy. But different governments and institutions still exhibit contrasting opinions on what type of geoeconomic strategy is most desirable. Classifications of economic diplomacy can be seen as falling on a continuum: at one end, states' full control over economic tools to further a comprehensive concept of national power; at the other end, looser forms of state backing for more narrowly conceived business opportunity.[2] The EU has struggled to stake out a clear, conceptually sound, and unified position on this continuum. Member states and the commission increasingly understand economic diplomacy in different ways. The return of geoeconomics to such preeminence is one of the most potent factors that has driven member states to adopt more competitive and even clashing international strategies. Notwithstanding the serious and necessary attention that policymakers now give to this area of policy, the EU as a whole struggles to articulate a balanced form of geoeconomics. While the EU needs to be more assertive and applied in advancing its geoeconomic interests, European governments risk becoming overly nefarious, mercantile bandwagoners.

A GEOECONOMIC WORLD

The Eurasia Group suggests that international economics is *the* central matter of global security today, supplanting the core dynamics of the post-9/11 era.[3] The emergence of a more geoeconomic world goes hand in hand with the much-commented on rise of "state capitalism." Such state capitalism is defined as being based on the lead role of para-statal agencies (owned wholly or in part by the government) and has been described as "the new norm" in global political economy.[4] The *Economist* detects a global rise of state capitalism, with many Western governments seduced by the apparent successes of this model in the rising powers and overlooking its weaknesses in generating innovation and allowing political freedom. And state capitalism runs inexorably beyond borders: it has a natural international extension as rising powers sew up deals with each other for the control of resources in exchanges outside the scope of the market.

Stephen King's widely read account of the financial crisis posits the euro meltdown as a major factor in pushing the world back toward zero-sum global geoeconomics. The rising powers of Asia have responded to the crisis in self-help mode and are less open to Western strictures about multilateral cooperation in which all sides win. The West's own crisis pushes other powers away from the very values with which the West has long sought to entice them. King maintains that the EU and wider crises have shoved the world peremptorily back toward "the world of the British East India Company," in which political control over resources is increasingly necessary for economic gain and the future is set to be a world of "smoke-filled rooms and questionable deals behind closed doors."[5] The implication is clear: the EU needs to adapt accordingly, not merely domestically but also in its global policies.

Dambisa Moyo concurs. She contends that the West cannot stick to liberal multilateralism when China and other states are playing by different rules. The liberal logic of comparative advantage does not work when some players seek absolute advantage and aim to maximize volumes of trade to control whole market segments. She opines that the West still has to adopt a tougher approach to deal with the "belligerent . . . ruthless" Rest. The West has been too soft and generous in allowing its companies to invest in rising powers in a way that mainly benefits those powers and in transferring intellectual property out of the West.[6] Many observers insist that the tensions associated with the euro crisis have shifted the weight of support away from mechanisms of shared governance. Since China joined the World Trade Organization (WTO) in December 2001, its mercantilism has intensified, not abated, with more generous state backing and credits provided to exporters. Fast-growing economies increasingly adhere to assertive policies to protect themselves from the European crisis. Parag Khanna thinks that the EU needs state-backed support for "aggressive commercial expansion," including through "buy European" campaigns.[7]

It is widely argued that a more geoeconomic world requires a more conditional stance on trade liberalization. Robert Skidelsky insists that a Keynesian solution to Europe's economic woes and broader global imbalances will require limits to trade and more domestically generated demand instead. If this is not pursued, he thinks that a complete disintegration of globalization is inevitable; debtor states, including those in the EU, will eventually opt for protectionism and devaluation. Interdependence is not so entrenched that it cannot be undone; it was deeper just prior to the 1930s Depression. Skidelsky insists that a more regulated and social democratic form of capitalism must involve Europe defending its own quality of life rather than supporting the kind of trade liberalization now sought by developing countries.[8]

Radical readings are even more categorical. They argue that the postcrisis switch to Keynesianism was not undertaken in a way that addresses the fundamental problems of over-accumulation, the "financialization" of capitalism, or economic imbalances at the international level. The emergence of a stronger state at the domestic level compounds Darwinian commercial competition and the problems of collective action at the global level, thus merely aggravating the international tensions that lie at the roots of the crisis.[9]

A crucial predicament flows from the rise of state capitalism elsewhere in the world: Does the "liberal West" meet fire with fire? Or does it try to douse the fire with more, not less, effort to enhance rules-based, cooperative, market solutions? It's one thing to make the case that, other things being equal, free markets are more likely than state capitalism to lead to efficient outcomes; it's quite another thing to determine how to respond when the countries practicing state capitalism appear to be gaining advantage and strategic control of assets by compromising the global functioning of market rules.

BETWEEN PROTECTIONISM AND RECIPROCITY

Against this background, three trends have defined EU trade policies since the beginning of the crisis: a rise in covert protectionism; a tilt toward reciprocity and away from unconditional market opening; and the search for bilateral or plurilateral trade accords, in preference to multilateral trade liberalization. Certainly, several aspects of EU foreign economic policy reflect a combative approach to the geoeconomic world. Many in Europe look at the apparently inexorable rise of state capitalism and, in effect, advocate for the option of meeting fire with fire. International economics are seen increasingly through the prism of political power, not merely the principles of mutually beneficial interdependence. Herman Van Rompuy has indeed recognized that "power and influence in the world are more and more a matter of economy, and less of weapons."[10] Europe has inched back toward something lightly akin to the concept of the "trading state" after a brief liberal period of the 1990s.[11] The trends corroborate suggestions that the (broadly liberal) European Commission has still not been able to establish more significant autonomy from member states when crucial tenets of foreign economic policy are at stake.[12]

Protectionism. Stephen Woolcock has traced the change in EU international trade policy through the crisis. He argues that the "peak of the liberal paradigm" in European economic diplomacy came in the late 1990s; that is, well before the current crisis. In the Doha multilateral trade round, by 2008 the EU was offering slightly greater reductions in agricultural tariffs and subsidies, before the United States and India fell out over safeguard measures. But member state eagerness for progress on investment, services, and intellectual property (the so-called Singapore issues) was never so strong as to encourage them to make really significant quid pro quo moves on agriculture. In 2010 the EU trade strategy changed tone and promised a more aggressive use of market access as a bargaining tool. Woolcock observes that in EU deliberations, the liberal states are now seen as the spoilers, not the protectionists. The argument thus holds sway that the EU must use its full market power by bargaining away trade access for concrete gain rather than adopting liberalization.[13]

After François Hollande's election victory, France's minister for industrial renewal was quoted as saying he would "engage unilateral protection measures for infant industries."[14] Just before the crisis, the French government effectively defined the national production of yogurt as a "strategic imperative" to protect Danone from foreign buyers. In October 2010 the high-profile Heseltine report, commissioned by the British government, advocated French-style blocks on foreign takeovers in some sectors in the UK.[15] Revealingly, Spain's Popular Party government has even given protectionism the label of "intelligent" trade policy.

Most postcrisis trade restrictions have been introduced in emerging powers. EU Trade Commissioner Karel De Gucht has complained regularly that postcrisis protectionism "has proven more persistent than was expected and seems to be further on the rise" because of measures adopted outside Europe.[16] But the EU overall is itself the fourth-highest user of new restrictions in the G20.[17] Global Trade Alert's reports on protectionism reveal a particularly notable increase in restrictive measures since 2012. By mid-2012, more than 300 restrictive measures had been imposed in each of the six largest member states since the start of the crisis.[18] Another study concludes that the EU has been guilty of operating more discriminatory trade measures than any other region or country.[19] Respected economists point out that, while the worst excesses of protectionism have been avoided, more subtle forms of behind-the-border restrictions are increasing faster in Europe than in any other region.[20] As one EU official rues, the introduction of myriad new regulations in response to the crisis has increased the specificity of EU rules and prompted a further divergence and separateness from international partners.

Trade officials admit that EU positions on trade have tightened because the judgment is that the EU can no longer accept the same asymmetry vis-à-vis rising powers as when Doha began more than a decade ago, now that the rising powers are so much more powerful and prosperous. Middle-income states have had trade preferences removed as a means of pressing them to conclude bilateral free trade agreements with the EU and have been subjected to new nontariff barriers. States have been excluded from the Generalized System of Preferences (GSP) on a simple GDP indicator, leaving China, Indonesia, and Thailand in but excluding weaker African states. In effect the EU narrows the group of states it deems "developing" in the WTO, reducing the breadth of access concessions. "Aid for trade" is now seen as an alternative to liberalization. There are also signs of a more protectionist stance toward green trade.[21] Additionally, new voting arrangements make it harder for member states to block trade-restrictive safeguard measures.[22]

The EU has deliberated on blocking takeovers from Chinese state-owned enterprises. One commissioner laments that member states are now nervous over Chinese takeovers even when they would not create any kind of dominant position in the states' domestic markets. Moreover, developed countries are now boosting spending in areas that have the least international "leakage" and that are most biased toward domestic producers.[23] Rising power diplomats complain about the impact of the ECB's cheap funding of EU banks on their own competitiveness. One significant cause of the dip in global trade in 2012 was the drying up of trade finance provided by European banks, previously responsible for more than a third of such funds essential to exporters, who are now obliged to narrow their focus to domestic markets.[24] After a decade of offshoring, officials now talk about the need for re-shoring production to Europe.

Reciprocity. Commission and member state trade officials reject the charge of protectionism. They point to the fact that trade flows have been sustained at high levels throughout the crisis and that the EU has pursued new deals on liberalization even during the worst of the recession. All of this contrasts with the decimation of global trade in the 1930s. Lessons have clearly been learned. Rather than imposing outright protection, the most significant shift in European policy has more subtly been toward the principle of "reciprocity." Officials report that this notion of reciprocity has become the commission's "new bible." In 2012 the EU introduced a new instrument that would make access to European procurement and other markets conditional upon China and other rising powers opening up their public procurement opportunities to European firms. The new measure allows governments to exclude non-EU bidders from procurement tenders if their own countries refuse to open their contracts to European bidders. Such political muscle also has been seen as necessary to deal with China's more assertive pressure on requiring technology transfer as part of its investment deals.

European Commission trade officials justify the measure, arguing that "we are so open we have no leverage." It is not a protectionist step, they insist, but a means of giving the EU more leverage to open markets and increase liberalization: "We need to be less altruistic, focus less on helping system conditions for others to prosper, and be more conditional in getting something concrete in return for market access." The EU, they suggest, cannot simply carry on as before when it is now "the only one who still believes in multilateralism." The official line is that reciprocity is aimed not to barricade the European economy but to open up China and other markets.

A fierce battle has ensued over the reciprocity regulation. This rather low-profile and technical-sounding innovation has concentrated tensions over the EU's postcrisis global identity. Under both the Sarkozy and Hollande administrations, the measure has been driven by France, apparently now ascendant over the normally liberal commission trade directorate. The French government has promised to "put foreign trade back in the service of employment." It will henceforth support only those trade agreements that are "clearly conducive to job creation in France [and] deal with nontariff barriers particularly that penalize French companies."[25] Spain has been a firm supporter of such conditions, under both socialist and conservative governments. Even the more liberal Mario Monti supported the measure during his tenure as Italian premier. The UK, the Netherlands, and smaller northern states have been more ambivalent, arguing for a lighter form of reciprocity. The British argument has been that while the regulation is not unreasonable in principle, it could easily be used for protectionist ends. Germany has questioned the proposal, although some detect it tilting toward the French line. As of late 2013, no generalized reciprocity provisions had been introduced into new formal legislation, but the broad principle is now prominent in the general approach to external economic policy.

Indeed, notwithstanding the doubts harbored by some governments, the trend has continued toward tighter reciprocity and away from unconditional, unilateral market liberalization. Until the early 2000s, EU trade policy was about deepening competition-oriented rules at the global level; it is now more focused on negotiating market access in select large economies.

For example, member states pushed the commission to negotiate a deal with China on solar panels, which gives Chinese suppliers a much lower minimum price than the commission had said was acceptable in European markets. In the autumn of 2013, the commission also pushed back action on a telecom case while it sought to secure a similar deal: dropping WTO action in return for negotiating European companies a significant share of a new Chinese 4G tender. In both cases, negotiated political deals have been preferred to pursuing firmer legal rules.

Some experts argue that tough, interest-driven reciprocity is needed not only against China but also against India.[26] In October 2012 the commission presented an update of EU industrial policy that promised to strengthen the use of reciprocity to create more level playing fields for European investors overseas and to back this up with a "raw materials diplomacy" to secure access to vital supplies.[27] In April 2013 the commission proposed a further set of measures to counter dumped and subsidized goods, promising a more aggressive use of tariffs on imports and a widened scope to retaliate without waiting for complaints from companies.

The *Economist's* Charlemagne categorized the reciprocity measure not so much as a trade-enhancing political lever but more as emblematic of a new spirit of protectionism. While the commission insists the new instrument will temper the bilateral resort to protectionism, in fact it will legitimize just this.[28] Global Trade Alert categorizes the measure as "cloak and dagger" protectionism.[29] Liberal states point out that the EU could hardly berate President Barack Obama's Buy America campaign if it then created what was in effect its own Buy Europe initiative. Reciprocity runs contrary to the focus on rigor and competitiveness that has dominated discussions over domestic policy linked to the euro crisis. The leading EU employers' forum, Business Europe, has assailed possible legislation as anticompetitive and contrary to the spirit of the WTO's Government Procurement Agreement. In that the EU is party to the agreement, there could be legal ramifications should the EU take unilateral actions against contract bidders from other signatory states.

Bilateral trade accords. In addition to protectionism and reciprocity, the third dimension of foreign economic policy is that trade liberalization efforts have switched to a plurilateral route from the multilateral level. This reflects an emergent approach within forums such as the G20: the aim is to build more ad hoc and shifting groupings of states on an issue-by-issue basis. Bilateral talks have produced some notable gains, notably in the form of free trade deals with South Korea, Central America, Peru, and Colombia. Negotiations for an EU-U.S. trade deal have commenced, overcoming reluctance due to the economic crisis on both sides of the Atlantic (the two still account for one-third of global trade). Crucially, business leaders have come to back this deal as WTO talks have remained stuck. A new deal was concluded with Canada in October 2013. The next chapter details the raft of bilateral accords being advanced in Asia.

However, several of these bilateral deals have hit problems. French protectionist instincts have come out clearly in discussions over exemptions to the EU-U.S. free trade mandate, the so-called Transatlantic Trade and Investment Partnership (TTIP). In the early stage of negotiations, France has managed to exclude a number of sectors, including cultural products and agriculture. In the autumn of 2013, it sought to limit the scope of new foreign investment dispute mechanisms in the TTIP. All this has engendered a fierce war of words between the commission and French ministers, the latter defending a broader principle of protectionism as vital to economic recovery.

THE RISE OF COMMERCIAL DIPLOMACY

Alongside these trends in trade policy, European governments have begun to back their own national companies in a far more explicit, political, and preferential way in the search for export and investment contracts. More specifically focused than general trade and investment policy, "commercial diplomacy" refers to diplomatic activity designed to advance commercial gain. European governments have long engaged in such activity, but the crisis has prompted them to intervene in support of commercial possibilities in a more direct, formalized, and systematic manner. In this sense, the EU has not reverted to wholesale, old-style, protectionist-based economic nationalism, so much as a subtler economic patriotism that attempts to "shape markets" to privilege the global interests of European firms, through varied types and combinations of "partial interventionism" and "strategic liberalization."[30]

Nearly all member states have embarked upon new strategies of commercial diplomacy. Even one self-declared liberal, northern member state's Europe minister alludes to a "feeling that economics is running foreign policy now" and concurs that "state muscle" is needed to back up businesses. A European commissioner notes that in internal discussions on commercial policy, the "mood is very strongly toward member states picking winners" specifically to compete in and with emerging economies. One member state director of economic diplomacy insists that a postcrisis focus on geoeconomics has provided the best means to temper European decline by prioritizing relations with rising powers. And indeed, nearly all member states now conduct a higher share of their total trade outside the EU than when the crisis started.

Even development funding is increasingly "blended," mixing aid with more commercially oriented credits; "beyond aid" strategies are shorthand for improving access for investment in developing countries. UN Development Program officials report that EU support for social protection aid projects is now being diverted covertly to shore up commercial interests. More loosely, the ECB's more relaxed policy is seen to be part of a geoeconomic strategy of bringing down the euro relative to the currencies of rising powers. There has been debate in Brussels and Frankfurt about market intervention to lower the value of the euro as a means of boosting exports, in a mercantile strategy for recovery.

Member states have pursued economic diplomacy in different forms. German state bodies plan for a strategic concept of economic competitiveness; the French government tends to a narrower diplomatic backing of national champions to secure contracts in global markets; the UK, the Netherlands, and the Nordic countries have become more geoeconomic but are slightly more reluctant for state strategies to cut across multilateral rules overtly.[31] The commission has been increasingly exercised about having to prevent member states from bending rules to create national champions as part of their global export drives. While the Lisbon Treaty enshrines a commitment to wrap bilateral investment treaties into single EU deals, in practice the focus on geoeconomics has tipped the scales even more toward bilateralism and away from common EU approaches. Competition is increasing between member states for commercial access to emerging markets. This has not been accompanied by coordination measures of equal weight at the EU level. Member states are more often going it alone in their quest for lucrative deals. Support for common EU mechanisms to seek debt purchases or investment contracts has not been forthcoming.

Germany has come to be seen as the archetype of geoeconomic power.[32] In 2012 it was the second-largest source of foreign direct investment (FDI) globally. Germany, not China, has the largest current account surplus in the world in proportionate terms. Many judge that Germany has positioned itself to be a "global middle power" rather than being restricted to an equal weighting with France and the UK through the steadfast anchor of an EU bloc. Chancellor Merkel's trade and investment efforts have increasingly and conspicuously been oriented toward China, through a flurry of high-level visits, investment delegations, and trade fairs. Germany has been more and more willing to offer a geostrategic quid pro quo to investment deals; between 2005 and 2010, Germany's arms exports doubled.[33] It negotiated bilaterally with China to agree on standards for electric cars and associated renewables-related trade, without bothering to coordinate at the EU level. Germany also struck bilateral deals with Kazakhstan and Mongolia on access to rare earths in response to China's restrictions on exports, undercutting parallel EU efforts.[34]

Many officials lament in private that Berlin's foreign policy vision is now almost exclusively a geoeconomic one. It has permitted an effective devaluation of salaries in order to preserve exports—a classical foundation for mercantilism. One of Germany's fears in the crisis was that a sizable appreciation of the euro would follow the exit of weaker member states. Chancellor Merkel has explicitly insisted that Germany should not sacrifice its export strength for the sake of correcting imbalances destabilizing the eurozone.[35]

In the UK, an overtly commercially led foreign policy has been pursued under the Conservative-led coalition government. Foreign Secretary William Hague has restructured the Foreign Office around a preeminently trade focus, in particular through creating a strikingly large Commercial and Economic Diplomacy Department. Ostensibly free market Britain has moved toward more overt government backing to raise export and FDI shares in global markets, helping companies more directly to win "high-value opportunities" and forming strategic partnerships with the main potential buyers. The government identifies poor export performance as one of the main "drags" on aggregate demand in Britain over the previous decade and now makes the case for state support to "correct market failures" and overtake the investment shares gained by competitors.[36] The British government has produced a white paper on commercial diplomacy, promising new export finance products and systematic political lobbying for large-scale contracts.[37] The Foreign Office also initiated a Charter for Business that laid out the key principles of a commercial diplomacy and indicated that businesses would be given more influence over foreign policy decisions.[38] David Cameron instructed ambassadors around the world to report on what they had done to back British business. The Labour opposition has regularly criticized the government for reducing foreign policy to trade policy. Philip Stephens offers an arresting historical parallel: the tone of British foreign policy has become distinctly Elizabethan in its national quest for overseas lucre.[39]

The prime minister led the UK's biggest-ever trade delegation to India; follow-up trips by Indian ministers secured the largest-ever joint investment packages between the two countries, worth more than five billion euros. There has been a dramatic increase in UK trade and investment missions and activity across Central Asia, with trade and investment flows to the region increasing through the crisis.[40] David Cameron led a business delegation on a high profile trip to Kazakhstan in June 2013, with British companies negotiating nearly a billion euros' worth of contracts. The UK now strives to be "the Gulf's commercial partner of choice": a network of new bilateral accords has been constructed across the region to back British businesses in winning contracts over the competition. The government has set ambitious targets to increase trade to the Gulf by two-thirds by 2015—a region to which the UK already exports more than to China.[41] In November 2012, David Cameron made a second extensive trip round the Gulf, to build on the 20 percent increase in exports to the region registered in 2011. He backed a BAE bid for a new five-year aircraft supply deal with Saudi Arabia. In the United Arab Emirates (UAE) he lobbied explicitly in favor of a possible $10 billion contract for Typhoon fighters against French and U.S. competition. And when he returned again to Oman only one month later, he announced a three-billion euro deal for BAE Systems to supply the Omani government with twelve Eurofighter and eight Hawk jets. BAE is now more dependent on the Gulf, and Saudi contracts in particular, as new procurement contracts within Britain itself dry up.

One well-placed journalist reports that British ministers have increasingly questioned the global public goods that the EU often proclaims as its purpose and instead use the union as one tool among several layers of action to deliver on tangible economic interests.[42] The perception that the EU is becoming more protectionist is certainly one factor among many that nourishes British views of the UK as a stand-alone free trader, with myriad commercial links no longer granting preferential treatment to other European markets. The UK runs a big trade deficit with the EU but a big trade surplus with the rest of the world; this is feeding pressure in the British Parliament for a foreign policy more oriented toward emerging economies. After his visits to India and the Gulf, when Cameron made a similar trip to Indonesia with a score of business leaders in tow, Chancellor of the Exchequer George Osborne made a subsequently much-cited string of observations: the fourth most populous country on earth currently buys less than 0.2 percent of Britain's exports; Britain exports more to Ireland than to Brazil, Russia, India, and China put together; and all this was the road to "economic irrelevance."[43] The UK has ostentatiously resurrected the commonwealth framework as a way of tapping into emerging markets.

France's predilection for active state-backed commercial diplomacy is of much longer vintage. The Hollande government has significantly increased export financing. French ministers have said that their renewed enthusiasm for sovereign wealth funds is in part emulation of one pillar of Chinese state capitalism. France has won huge contracts to supply India with pressured reactors, even while a common EU nuclear agreement has remained blocked. In one example emblematic of how economic dynamics now appear to override political sensitivities, during his state visit to Algeria in December 2012, François Hollande negotiated a deal for the French carmaker Renault to build an assembly plant near Oran.

The Spanish government has also given its embassies a "specifically economic mandate." Marca España (Trademark Spain) has been defined as the guiding principle of the People Party's foreign policy. The government has more overtly used King Juan Carlos to capture big financing deals in Qatar and the UAE to help with the needed recapitalization of Spanish banks. In this way it also won train contracts in Saudi Arabia and Kazakhstan; the one in Kazakhstan was worth 1 billion euros over fifteen years. Spain posted record exports in 2012. One official notes that the whole Foreign Affairs Ministry has been mobilized for commercial gain. Spain's Casa Árabe has switched its focus to economic diplomacy at the behest of the government; the agency's whole mission is now framed in terms of economic interests.

The Italian Foreign Ministry has launched an "economic diplomacy" initiative, coordinating the international commercial activities of other ministries and increasing export finance, especially for small and medium-sized enterprises.[44] Denmark has created a post of minister for trade and investment within the Ministry of Foreign Affairs; this is seen as the main Danish response to the crisis, with the ministry committing to intervene more directly to help Danish companies win contracts. Individual commercial partnerships have been developed with each of the BRIC countries.[45] The Netherlands has put in place a new commercial diplomacy strategy and is looking at means of improving the effectiveness of Dutch embassies' support for businesses.[46] In his investiture speech in November 2012, Dutch Prime Minister Mark Rutte named economic diplomacy as his government's top international priority and announced the creation of a fund to direct investment toward developing markets.[47] Poland is exploring the "globalization of Polish foreign policy," with the aim of securing better economic gains beyond Europe.[48]

The result of all this bilateral commercial diplomacy is an increasingly fierce rivalry among member states in emerging markets. The UK was furious that India opted for French Rafale jets rather than the Typhoon, developed by a number of European companies. A ferocious and opaque competition ensued for a high-speed train contract in Morocco: Siemens complained that its more competitive bid was sunk by the French government deploying elite connections with the palace and entering into a host of shady strategic trade-offs to secure the deal for France's TGV. Italy stirred up classically geoeconomic ructions with Austria and some northern states when it resolutely backed the so-called Trans Adriatic Pipeline (TAP) into southern Italy against the ill-fated Nabucco pipeline that would have run into central European markets.

Diplomats acknowledge that there is no thinking on where there might be economies of scale in member states joining forces on commercial diplomacy or helping to secure contracts for each other. Member states have not coordinated their rules on limiting FDI in strategic sectors. Diplomats observe that fiercer competition among member states is a spillover from the perception that Germany is looking out for its narrow national interests amid the EU's internal crisis. Experts talk of a new scramble for investment and energy opportunities in Africa, with EU member states competing with each other, as well as with Chinese, South African, Indian, Brazilian, and Malaysian companies. Work on a more common EU-level commercial diplomacy strategy has stalled.

A BALANCED GEOECONOMICS

It is not unreasonable that postcrisis external EU policies have been driven by material interest. European leaders are right to argue that emerging from the crisis requires the EU to be more assertive in pursuing its commercial interests globally. The apparent successes of state capitalism present a genuine challenge: previously statism was largely antimarket, but it now seems to navigate the global marketplace with surety and confidence. The EU cannot ignore this reality. However, international economic policy must be crafted within a framework that dovetails far more tightly with the broader gamut of geostrategic objectives. This will ensure that a benign form of geoeconomics takes shape. To wit, the EU needs a form of geo-economic multilateralism rather than zero-sum bilateralism. The EU's own leverage depends on the survival of multilateral economic principles.

There are signs that European governments have inched toward an admirably balanced form of geoeconomics. In this regard, the nuanced changes to the EU's internal economic model have informed the evolu-tion of external policies. As outlined in chapter two, in terms of domestic economic policy, European governments have sought targeted change but within the broad parameters of existing social market principles. To some degree, the same balanced perspective is evident at the international level. The EU has aimed to design policies that are motivated by a more results-driven search for commercial gain, without the excesses of rules-weakening statecraft or the most purist form of realpolitik control. Geoeconomics have not entirely eclipsed other dimensions of EU policy. Political and security policies in some circumstances still prevail. Relative to internal EU flows, European global trade and investment remain modest. While there has been something of a geoeconomic stampede to Asia, the economic aspects of EU policies have, if anything, weakened in Latin America. In the Middle East and sub-Saharan Africa, trade and investment efforts have intensified but still underplay these regions' full potential. More EU effort is certainly warranted as part of a postcrisis external strategy. A stronger thrust of economic realism pervades European external policy, but EU member states have still not mobilized economic instruments as the pri-mary source of power in emerging markets.[49]

The EU has not abandoned rules-based multilateralism. It is suspended somewhere in between enthusiastic reliance on liberal interdependence and zero-sum survival mode. While EU member states are more aggressively pursuing investment and bilateral trade deals, they are not approaching geo-economics in the same kind of direct way that China and, to a lesser extent, the United States plan for control over the strategic resources and transport nodes of the global system. German diplomats insist that Germany is not a narrowly geoeconomic power but is committed to using its commercial presence to deepen rules-based global processes. Indeed, Germany has not become so geoeconomic as to deploy hard power for economic gain.[50] Dutch diplomats see their main value as being to improve the institutional and policy context for investment rather than negotiating individual deals with local officials.[51] In its Caspian pipelines strategy, the EU tried a more classic geoeconomic quest for "spatial control" by backing the Nabucco project, but this failed, as the latter was abandoned in mid-2013. European energy companies have backed other, Russia-run options on the basis of economic calculations; and while Nabucco has now been discarded, China quickly built a connection to Turkmenistan. The European Commission stepped back from direct support for Nabucco as many companies and governments insisted that other pipeline options were more attractive.

While there is much virtue in this balance of European strategy, postcrisis approaches to global economic interests have not generally been framed in a comprehensive fashion. In relation to the various possible economic diplomacy strategies, most governments have tilted toward a narrowly instrumental, knee-jerk commercial diplomacy rather than a carefully planned and comprehensive economic statecraft that conceives strategic interests in the round. It is not clear that such commercial diplomacy is working. In at least some places the EU is in danger of becoming a mere suppliant for commercial contracts. This may produce important and immediate material gains, but it also breeds a perception that the EU's external vision is increasingly and unduly constricted. One official worries that European governments are winning contracts by "cashing in on political relations, not winning contracts on price or quality" and that this approach can work only a small number of times before the political capital is spent.

The scramble for exports has arguably deflected from the importance of correcting depressed domestic demand within Europe for long-term competitiveness. Overall, exports have proven resilient during the crisis, as demand increases from rising economies. However, despite enhanced commercial diplomacy, in most markets European companies are struggling to hold off stiff competition across all sectors from non-Western producers. There is a plethora of initiatives that the EU has failed to move forward in more tangible and substantive terms. These include outstanding free trade talks in Asia and Latin America, where Mercosur has refused to accept European terms; energy projects in the Caspian; and recently formulated strategic policy frameworks in the southern Mediterranean and sub-Saharan Africa. Sterling has depreciated by nearly a third since the beginning of the crisis without major improvement in the UK's trade performance.

While a degree of reciprocity in trade policy is desirable, the EU risks deploying the notion in a manner that simply scuppers beneficial liberalization. Its new reciprocity clause will be extremely difficult to apply with wise balance: it is somewhat counterintuitive not to do what you believe is good for oneself in order to press others to change their behavior. If pursued too hard, this approach risks being self-defeating. It reinforces the perception that the EU may be a reasonably important trading partner but that it has little political intent to uphold international rules. Overly tough conditions of reciprocity in trade talks are likely to backfire. While French diplomats insist that firm reciprocity is essential to a "more balanced approach to trade," some other, newer, and less wealthy member states protest that this risks choking off investment flows that they more urgently need. The BusinessEurope president has pointed out why strong-arm trade tactics may prove conceptually ill-conceived in an era of interlinked company structures: "We have to be careful about bashing Chinese exports to Europe—over 50 percent [of these] come from our own companies."[52] Hard-bargaining reciprocity harbors a contradiction: it presumes that the best way to correct the EU's loss of material power is by exerting material bargaining pressure—the very thing it is losing. Reciprocity may be appropriate but only when it is pursued in a more diffuse fashion. The EU will need to ensure that this new philosophy does not cut a self-inflicted wound.

The opening of bilateral trade talks sets up states in the same region as rivals for access to European markets, undermining their commitment to intra-regional coordination. It sits uneasily with the EU's claim that strong regionalism is a vital building block of multilateralism. The EU points out that to compensate for the rise of bilateral talks, it has increased technical support for regional capacity building to the Association of Southeast Asian Nations (ASEAN) and other groupings—but this is relatively limited fare. In Asia and other regions, plurilateralism is often damned as a venal Western divide-and-rule strategy. Asians and also the Brazilian government have expressed discontent with the likely distortionary effects of the TTIP.

The notion of state-oriented capitalism goes hand in hand with an expansion in the number of "strategic sectors" closed to foreign investment and a race to lock down control over resources globally. But this is an expensive way to access supplies, and the intricate deals needed are difficult to sustain over the long term. Better financial regulation certainly needs strong state rules, not just abstract, common multilateral standards. But European governments err in linking this to subtle forms of covert protectionism. Production is now organized globally; the EU was formed when for many companies regional interdependence was the limit of ambition and scale. The UK especially cannot shut itself off from the global economy: to cover its huge level of combined private, commercial, and public debt (second in the world to the United States), it depends on holdings of foreign assets. The crisis renders a European globalism more necessary, not redundant.

A successful international economic strategy will require a very finely balanced recalibration of European economic policy. Markets still undoubtedly require more effective taming, but beefed-up state regulation should not eviscerate other elements of economic internationalism. While a more equitable globalization is surely needed, European governments have begun to "tame global markets" in a way that protects their own engrained positions, not so as to give weaker states a better deal. A "decoupling" from the U.S. economy is not possible. Growth potential in a large part of the eurozone will continue to be low if the international dimension of the so-called EU2020 strategy—which commits the union to become more globally competitive—does not have more of an impact than its predecessor Lisbon strategy. The increased hesitancy to advance with the internal EU market in services undercuts European global competitiveness in a range of vital sectors.

Enhancing strategic presence will quite properly involve seeking short-term, bilaterally negotiated benefits, but these are better conceived as staging posts toward deeper multilateralism than as final destinations in themselves. Bilateral trade deals are indeed positive, insofar as they are WTO-approved. But firmer evidence is required that they are actually fashioned so as to be stepping-stones toward multilateral progress, as the EU claims. Some senior diplomats worry that the EU's tough reciprocal economic bargaining is undermining fundamental multilateral principles. As one very highly placed EAS diplomat acknowledges: "Going bilateral is raising systemic worries." Noted trade expert Jean-Pierre Lehmann says that the EU is disingenuous to argue that it is pursuing bilateral accords merely to keep liberalization alive when others are blocking the Doha

Round. Its own actions, he contends, have contributed to Doha's failure; its own swing to bilateralism is a cause, not just an effect, of multilateralism's paralysis.[53]

Aggressive mercantilism and tit-for-tat commercial bargaining flow from the assumption that competitive multipolarity will now dominate the global order. However, while state-centered multipolarity will be one feature of the post-Western world order, it would be unduly oversimplifying to paint it as the sole or overwhelmingly defining dynamic. Polarity implies a degree of separateness between blocs that is simply not attainable today. It is now widely recognized that the most influential features of the new world order are speed, unpredictability, deepening problem intersections at all levels, multi-actor networks, and nonlinear change, all quite antithetical to the staid frameworks of traditional, inter-pole diplomacy.[54] According too much weight to multipolarity can smack of structural determinism. One of the main trends is the rise of a "global middle class," even as the European professional class is squeezed. Individual empowerment over the state increases even as state capitalism takes hold.

Ian Bremmer judges that geoeconomically driven "state capitalism" is winning unwarranted admiration in the West. Western governments will not go as far as explicitly espousing state capitalism, but the pull is certainly in the direction of more government-controlled markets. Bremmer argues that too many in the West are now overly positive about the notion of state capitalism. They fail to realize, he argues, that systems containing elements of state capitalism will not stay strong over the long term. This is because ultimately they operate markets for national, political interests that take precedence over efficiency, innovation, and equitable distribution, or indeed over the notions of civic freedom that should underpin economic activity.[55]

An overly instrumental geoeconomics is unlikely to prove sustainable. The crisis has led to a more commercial diplomacy but has simultaneously hampered such an approach by denying companies the credit they need for investment abroad. The irony is that the appeal of state capitalism has proven enticing just when EU states' funds to channel behind such an approach are so limited. The EU has invested much hope in a series of formalized strategic partnerships signed with rising powers. The crisis certainly requires the EU to rethink who is a "strategic" partner and who is not. But these bilateral partnerships are far from being a panacea. The sobering truth is that the EU now defines many partners as "strategic" without their seeing the EU the same way in return.

Several writers have expressed concern that the EU's external strategies are currently too "narrow" to represent a sophisticated pursuit of economic interests. European commercial diplomacy is a concept designed almost to take politics out of the equation, while U.S. economic statecraft is used to underpin American global strategic leadership.[56] Jonas Parello-Plesner laments "Germany's inept strategic culture . . . drifting away in extra-European flirtations with BRIC-identities."[57] Katinka Barysch highlights how little an ultra-pragmatic, economically driven approach has achieved in relations with Russia.[58] The payoffs for reciprocal deals are proving dear. The UAE made the EU pay for its purchase of Airbus aircraft with a political agreement to cede more routes to Emirate carriers. European private sector executives admit they are at an early stage in working through how the broader international repercussions of the crisis affect geoeconomic cost-benefit analysis.[59]

After the ravages of the crisis, the EU can no longer compete simply on quantitative measures of trade volumes and market shares. Instead it must focus on setting the conditions that its niche areas of competition require to flourish.[60] It is unrealistic to think that member states will desist entirely from bilateral investment initiatives when these can deliver quicker and more concrete gain, and when opportunities in rising markets dilute the absolute privilege accorded to intra-European alliances. But the EU has done little to anchor the agility of such bilateralism more firmly in a framework of shared interest that minimizes mutually harmful commercial aggression among member states. Denmark and other smaller countries have begun to realize that their own commercial diplomacy depends on the EU level, as they have won much BRIC business on the basis of subcontracting through larger European economies.[61] There are differences among member states: while most at least frame their discourse in terms of common European interests vis-à-vis large rising powers, even as they chase bilateral contracts, the UK is more instrumental in conceiving the EU level as desirable only when it serves tangible national interests.

CONCLUSION

In sum, a clear legacy of the economic crisis is that the EU has come to invest greater effort to strengthen its diplomatic policies to underpin geo-economic interests. However, top officials in the European Council and EAS admit there is still no conceptual framework for relating geoeconomics to political interests. Geoeconomics comes in different hues: EU member states have begun to deploy political tools for narrowly defined economic interests, but they have shown less foresight in deploying economic tools for broader political interests. Arguably, geoeconomics should play to the traditional EU strength of being an "economic giant." But in many regions it also reveals its Achilles' heel of an abiding disconnect between economic and geopolitical interests. While European governments are justified in their more determined pursuit of geoeconomic interests, they still need to develop a fully comprehensive and political understanding of what those interests rightfully entail.

CHAPTER 5

ASIA'S PENINSULA?

A t the end of 2010, a Reflection Group of notables evocatively warned that the EU risked being reduced to the "increasingly irrelevant West-ern peninsula of the Asian continent."[1] Of a piece with the drift this conjured up, the economic crisis has indeed strengthened Asia's influence over Europe. Some observers go as far as suggesting that the tables have turned and that the pertinent question now is to assess Asia's power over Europe, not European influence in Asia. However, the eurozone crisis has also had the more positive effect of finally prompting the EU to correct its relative neglect of Asia, as European governments have scrambled to avoid marginalization from the supposed Asian century. Many significant and well-designed new initiatives have been introduced to inject substance into EU-Asia relations. While Asia's influence has undoubtedly solidified, in some areas a more benign and trust-building relationship of mutual inter-dependence has taken shape between Asia and Europe. Yet, unsurprisingly, on some policies tensions have arisen, while the EU still equivocates over a sufficiently comprehensive engagement in Asia. The crisis has intensified Europe's turn to Asia; what this means for power dynamics between the two regions remains far from straightforward.

THE END OF NEGLECT

The EU has long been criticized for being too narrow, expedient, and ad hoc in its approach to Asia.[2] Diplomats agree in private that the EU has not previously engaged with Asia geostrategically in the same manner and depth as the United States. The EU has for many years exhibited little strategic perspective in Asia beyond a race for commercial contracts. The general consensus berated the EU for reacting tardily and underwhelmingly to Asia's rise. Kishore Mahbubani, a virulent critic, insisted that the "biggest strategic flaw in the EU's policies toward Asia is the assumption that these policies can continue on autopilot, even when the world is changing rapidly and Asia keeps rising so steadily … if Europe could think and act strategically, it would be busy knocking on Asian doors."[3] An apparent legacy of misunderstanding has weighed down one of the EU's least prioritized sets of external relations.

On the back of the financial crisis, this low-profile passivity has gradually given way to belated European efforts to catch up with Asia's ascendance. The concern with recapturing presence in Asia is in fact not new. As far back as 1994 the EU published a New Asia Strategy that predicted the continent's rise to preeminence and recognized the imperative that Europe correct its disregard of the region. This strategy was accorded several upgrades well before the eurozone crisis began. The Asia-Europe Meeting process commenced in 1996, a tangible product of a reinforced diplomatic focus on Asia. Officials insisted that this process was a success in attracting a high level of leader participation, and that its loose dialogue method imbued useful flexibility. However, the rather dispersed and intermittent substantive improvements to European policies belied these and many other formal declarations of Asia's rising importance. The Asia-Europe Meeting flitted between "topics of the day" with little concrete geostrategic vision or commitment. There was little or no follow-through on announcements of a trade facilitation initiative, an investment promotion action plan, and an environmental technology center.[4] Asian states continued to focus on select European states, not the EU per se, and also not in a notably strategic fashion.

The crisis has undoubtedly corrected Europe's inattention to Asia. As Europe's crisis has spiraled and Asia's star continues to rise, the EU has issued plentiful commitments to a new beginning in its relationship with Asia. Such were the rush of ministerial visits to and crush of high-level meetings with the continent that the EU declared 2012 its "Year of Asia." Catherine Ashton insisted that "developing our relations with Asia across the board is a major strategic objective. Put simply … Europe and Asia need each other."[5] The high representative began her "Asian semester." As the United States made its high-profile "pivot" or "rebalance" to Asia, European diplomats engineered a more understated "mini-pivot." Officials frame the distinction thus: "The U.S. will be an Asian power. We will be an Asian partner."[6] On a 2012 visit to Malaysia, David Cameron declared that decades of British "benign neglect" were over. In late 2012, Foreign Secretary William Hague claimed that "Britain is looking East as never before."[7] The French defense minister likewise declared at the Shangri-La Dialogue, an annual intergovernmental forum on security, that his country would no longer be guilty of underplaying Asia's importance.[8]

A first EU-ASEAN Business summit was held in 2011. In both 2010 and 2012 more effort was put into the biannual Asia-Europe Meeting, due to the twin prompts of the crisis and the U.S. rebalancing to Asia.[9] In addition, April 2012 witnessed a striking revival of EU-ASEAN relations, with a beefed-up action plan sealing deeper cooperation between the two organizations. Catherine Ashton led the largest-ever delegation of EU officials to an EU-ASEAN ministerial dialogue that promised deeper institutional ties on everything from counterterrorism to trade. The EU acceded to the ASEAN Treaty of Amity and Cooperation, which opened the possibility of being included in the East Asia Summit. Member states' bilateral agreements have multiplied. For example, Germany established bilateral, strategic partnerships with Vietnam and Indonesia in 2012, moving beyond its traditional partners in the region.

Perhaps the most significant aspect of renewed effort lies in the EU's push to sign a raft of new bilateral trade deals. This constitutes a belated response to the battery of trade accords offered by the United States and China across Asia in the early 2000s—a time when the EU was still keen to prioritize the multilateral Doha round. The EU dropped its attempt to sign a region-to-region trade deal as it grew frustrated with ASEAN's inability to make progress on common positions on trade. The EU-ASEAN free trade area was scuppered for several reasons. The EU did not want to include Cambodia, Laos, or Burma, for a mix of developmental and human rights reasons. Poorer ASEAN states were not in a position to accept EU strictures on opening up services and investment sectors or on intellectual property. In response, and thinking primarily of the imperative of recouping ground in Asia, the EU overturned its own rules against bilateral trade deals. Bilateral talks seemed better able to unblock progress. For the EU it was more fruitful to pursue tangible benefits individually with Singapore and Malaysia.[10]

The EU concluded its most far-reaching trade deal with South Korea in 2011. This has strongly benefited EU exports. The EU accounted for 40 percent of FDI to Korea in 2012, while exports increased by more than 30 percent. A free trade accord with Singapore was finalized in December 2012. A mandate was then reached for negotiations to commence with Japan. Negotiations for a similar agreement with Thailand were launched in March 2013. Exploratory talks were open at various stages with Vietnam, Malaysia, the Philippines, and Taiwan. In June 2012, Ashton traveled to Islamabad to sign a new EU-Pakistan five-year Engagement Plan. Meanwhile, the EU has continued to push for a free trade agreement with India despite the crisis; if enacted, this would be the biggest liberalizing project to date.

For their part, Asian states hope that bilateral deals with the EU will serve as a counterweight to their increasing trade dependence on China. Ironically indeed, China is the one state in Asia that has to date pressed to maintain a multilateral route to its trade relations with Europe. European Union officials insist that their raft of new bilateral offers improves the prospect of overarching multilateral liberalization, to the extent that each bilateral offer encourages other partners to offer similar market-opening deals.

The EU and Asia are each other's biggest trading partners. The crisis has notably intensified Europeans' commercial tilt toward Asia. The EU has done better than the United States in retaining export shares of Asian markets. In ASEAN states the EU has lost a small amount of market share, from 11 percent in 2000 to 10 percent in 2010; this was due to China's presence increasing spectacularly from 4 to 14 percent over the same period, while U.S. and Japanese shares fell below that of the EU. The EU's assertive economic diplomacy has helped ensure that European exports to Asia have surged ahead of imports from the region during the crisis.[11] The UK has become the second-largest investor in Indonesia. The crisis period has witnessed a remarkable rise in Indian purchases of large European companies.

The EU and China are now each other's second-largest commercial partners. European Union exports to China have continued to grow during the crisis, from 136 billion euros in 2010 to 143 billion euros in 2012. Because exports have increased faster than imports, the EU's trade deficit with China has narrowed. German exports to China have doubled since 2007. While China suspended high-level contacts with the British government after David Cameron met with the Dalai Lama, the UK's exports increased by 16 percent in 2012, more than any other major trading partner. UK Chancellor of the Exchequer George Osborne led a high-tech business trip to China in October 2013, which marked the resumption of economic dialogue.

Investment flows have risen dramatically. Between 2008 and 2011, Chinese investment in Europe increased tenfold, from 700 million euros in 2008 to 7.4 billion euros in 2011. A third of all Chinese foreign investment in 2011 went to EU states. A series of Chinese investments and takeovers has hit the headlines, including of the venerable Rover, Volvo, and Saab companies in the automobile sector, the likes of Thames Water among several energy-related stakes, and infrastructure hubs such as Athens's main port. In the first six months of 2012, the rate of investment growth accelerated even further, with Chinese investment to the EU increasing by a huge 63 percent.[12] Talks have begun on an EU-China investment treaty.

The EU has also consolidated its position as Asia's largest provider of development assistance. British aid, for example, is highly Asia-oriented, with India, Bangladesh, Pakistan, Afghanistan, and Nepal in its top twenty recipients, along with reasonably meaningful programs in Indonesia and Vietnam. Vietnam and Bangladesh are in the top ten of Danish aid recipients. The European Commission has promised to mold its aid profile in Asia more tightly to the EU's strategic turn to the region, such as by funding more interregional dialogues.[13] The EU released a new tranche of money for support of ASEAN regional integration in 2012.

Naturally, not all trends have been as positive as they might have been. Prominent Asian observers stress that despite all the recent improvements to the Asia-Europe Meeting, it remains essentially the same nebulous and informal talking shop that deliberately eschews tangible output.[14] The EU has to correct a deeply embedded legitimacy shortfall: for many years European leaders failed even to turn up at Asia-Europe Meetings, causing Asian participants to conclude that the forum has been of little value in reducing differences or generating the dynamics of positive socialization.[15] A common Asian view is that the EU has become overly anxious about China's rise and consequently still neglects to engage systematically with the rise of other Asian powers.[16] Asian diplomats lament that as of late 2013 the follow-through on the 2012 EU-ASEAN action plan remains extremely limited.

Trade talks with India, Japan, Taiwan, and Vietnam have all dragged on and have failed to produce the promised steps forward from their respective starting points. The EU-India accord, supposedly on the verge of conclusion for many years, remains blocked. The Japan free trade agreement mandate was cleared only in November 2012, after a prolonged scoping exercise and following pressure from France and others for a more restrictive negotiating remit. Talks remain stalled with Malaysia, have barely begun with the Philippines, and have failed to extend beyond a preliminary exploration of terms with much-undervalued Indonesia.

While overall trade between Europe and Asia has increased, its rate of growth slowed in 2012. The EU's trade deficit with ASEAN has remained constant at around 25 billion euros a year between 2007 and 2011. Indonesia's ambassador to the European Union points out that to complete its Asian awakening, the EU still needs to appoint a high-level representative for ASEAN, as the United States, China, and Japan have done.[17] (In 2013 the External Action Service has begun to look at whether this might be possible.)

Absolute levels of exchanges leave much room for improvement. At the end of 2012, the United States overtook the EU as the main destination for Chinese exports. The EU still invests less in China than in Norway. The EU still has far more invested in China than vice versa. Even after the growth in trade, in 2012 the EU only exported slightly more to China than to Switzerland. European investment in India is only half of that. The EU still needs to make a serious effort to catch up: China and six ASEAN states formed the world's largest free trade area in 2012.

POWER REVERSAL?

Asian states have long bridled at being treated as supposed subjects of European power. The relationship has traditionally been measured in terms of how much influence Europe exerted over Asia, whether such an impact was benign or harmful, and how far Asian regimes pushed back against it. In the wake of the crisis, this no longer seems the appropriate metric for measuring the EU-Asian relationship. The crisis has clearly not only diluted European power in Asia but also quite conspicuously intensified Asian sway over Europe. Several research projects have captured the fact that Asians today see Europe as weak and ineffective, rather than overly interfering.[18] The former Malaysian premier, the indomitable Mahathir Mohamed, was not immune to schadenfreude in pointing out that centuries of European strictures were over and that "the shoe is on the other foot now."[19]

The clearest sign of this power shift lies in European pleas for financial assistance. To help shore up the eurozone, Japan pledged $80 billion to the IMF; China pledged $43 billion and India $10 billion. One World Bank director believes that President Sarkozy's 2011 request for Chinese funds to save the euro represented a "historic event," such was its utter reversal of centuries of power dynamics.[20] Asia has become the largest holder of euro-denominated assets; by 2013 more than a quarter of the foreign exchange portfolio of Asia's major central banks was in euros.[21] When the EU asked outside powers to match its own 200 billion euro pledge to help stabilize the crisis, Asian governments were cautious. They recalled that in the dark days of their own financial crisis in 1997, they got little more than lectures and hard conditionality from European governments. While China did channel some money into the EU's rescue fund directly, it insisted on large-scale support going mainly through the IMF. From 2010 to 2012 Japan bought $7 billion worth of bonds issued by the eurozone's temporary rescue fund, 7 percent of the rescue bonds on issue; then in January 2013 it announced it would purchase bonds issued by the European Stability Mechanism as it offered securities for the first time.[22] China is thought to have bought around 1 trillion in euro-denominated assets. Some observers claim that China was the largest purchaser of Portuguese and Irish bailout bonds, before switching its attention to buying bonds in Germany and other surplus states (although there are no official figures to corroborate this).[23] At the EU-China summit in February 2012, the China Investment Corporation declined to invest in European debt, opting for a focus on infrastructure and company purchases.[24] Spanish Prime Minister José Luis Rodríguez Zapatero was an infrequent traveler but made four trips to China; by the time he left office in December 2011, more than a quarter of Spanish debt was held by rising powers. Ironically, democracy-resistant China cites the constraints of domestic opinion to justify its disinclination to help rich Europeans any further. And in terms of money going the other way, China itself will receive no more European Commission aid as of 2014. Trade Commissioner Karel De Gucht was clear on the new dynamics of the relationship: "We need the money."[25]

The Asian Development Bank stresses that the region has accumulated unprecedented levels of reserves and that the eurozone crisis has dramatically accelerated the breach between fast-growing intra-Asian trade flows and the declining share of trade with the United States and the EU.[26] Record capital flight out of many European markets found its flip side in strong capital flows into Asian markets, after the Asian markets suffered only a brief trough in 2008–2009.[27] Rising Asian powers have become less reliant on transfers of Western technology. Asia currently has a higher share of global research and development expenditure (31 percent) than Europe (25 percent). Asian powers have been far more assertive and explicit in linking a change in voting weights in international bodies to their support for overcoming the euro crisis. As a result of the crisis, China was able to increase its voting weight in the IMF and World Bank beyond that of any EU member state. Europe, it appears, is now *demandeur*, while Asia's interest is far less urgent or intense; it is the mirror image of the imbalance that existed during the 1990s and early 2000s.

While Asian governments still tend to complain about not being taken seriously by Europe, the huge number of European ministerial visits to Asia in 2012 contrasted with a pitifully small number of trips by senior Asian ministers coming the other way into Brussels.[28] Some policymakers lament that the United States has managed to get Asian states to take its debts seriously, and thus is able to carry on funding them at low interest rates, while the EU has had a harder time convincing Asian powers that its problems matter to them. While the EU's special adviser on ASEAN insists that the union's role still hinges around the attractiveness to Southeast Asian states of its own integration model, most observers concur that Asia represents a stark case of Europe's power-by-attraction now weakening.[29] The crisis has quite significantly reinforced ASEAN governments' open dislike of the EU model of integration. If anything, lesson learning is beginning to run the other way: as said, French ministers claimed that their enthusiasm for sovereign wealth funds as a means of enhancing state control over investments came from Asia.

Of course, the direction of influence seems to have changed most dramatically in relation to China. Martin Jacques argues that before the crisis China still needed Europe more than Europe needed China, but now it is patently the other way around. Even member states previously most resistant to allowing in Chinese companies are now searching for funds. China has bought government bonds, increased investments in European companies, and moved into European public procurement markets. In the wake of the crisis, China has been far more assertive in its push for a fundamentally reformed international financial system, even talking about convertibility of the renminbi—a crucial move that would transform international relations. Jacques invokes the startling irony: European governments that for many years advocated strict IMF conditionality on developing states and criticized Chinese engagement in Africa for circumventing such conditions now queue up in Beijing because Chinese loans come without the conditions attached to IMF loans.[30] Meanwhile, China's position could be termed disingenuous: it berates the EU for a lack of coordination and unity, but in the crisis it has benefited enormously from the ability to pick off cheap assets as member states have undercut each other.[31]

Another level at which the power inversion is felt is that European governments have come to court Asian powers for new trade and investment deals far more assiduously than vice versa. The EU has become more dependent on Asian trade, Asia less dependent on European trade. The EU has been the main advocate for trade liberalization in part because Asian states currently enjoy lower barriers into European markets than vice versa. The biggest six member states now have their own strategic partnerships with China, outdoing each other to raise the level of these dialogues. The German government has reached the level of holding de facto joint cabinet meetings with its Chinese and Indian counterparts. Germany's bilateral strategic partnership with China has roared ahead as the EU equivalent lumbers on with thinner substance. Even central European states have launched their own summits with China.

China judges there to be a shift in power within the EU and this has altered its own policy toward Europe. China is now the third-largest market for Germany's exports and based on current trends will soon overtake France and the United States to become the largest destination. Competition among member states means that the overall trade deficit with China is not approached as a problem of geopolitical dependence as much as in the United States: indeed, Germany is the one state that runs a surplus with China. China has long solicited the EU as a counterbalance to the United States. But the crisis means that an alliance with fellow surplus states has become a more natural frame of reference, with other EU states having more in common with the deficit-stricken United States. Business representatives regret that member states have undercut each other, driving down profit margins for all European bidders and leaving China with higher gains. Moreover, China has offered financial help and trade progress at the multilateral level, so it asks EU representatives why member states urge it to forget multilateralism and provide direct cash and deals on a bilateral, preferential basis.

Trends reflect Germany's strength but also a new dependency on Chinese demand for Berlin's own growth. Germany has a highly commercial view of the Chinese market—a "strategic parochialism" in the words of Hans Kundnani and Jonas Parello-Plesner. In contrast, China has approached Germany in a strategic sense, driving a wedge between its noninterventionist line on foreign and security matters and the United States, France, and the UK.[32] China has been actively enticed by the growing number of investment promotion agencies in member states, including at the subnational level. European governments are making much more effort to attract funds from China's sovereign wealth funds, and their strictures on the need for transparency in these funds are no longer heard.[33] Chinese investment has extended for the first time into strategically important areas of the EU economy, engendering concerns over "economic security."[34] European governments have courted investments from some of the Chinese firms that the United States has prohibited on the grounds of security concerns. Policymakers say that European interests now hinge on encouraging China toward a more consumption-oriented growth model that could rebalance trade with the EU.

China has begun on occasion to exert power in a much more direct fashion. It threatened to cancel an order for 45 Airbus planes if the EU insisted on imposing air fuel taxes on Chinese planes; for a variety of reasons, the union postponed the tax. China has been clearer on what its priority demands are from the EU: for the union to grant it "market economy status" and lift the arms embargo in place since 1989. China's assertiveness and nationalism have increased, not diminished, as European governments have raced to build up commercial portfolios. China is changing its favored European partners from year to year and beginning to play them off against each other in Putinesque fashion. It has even gained ground in the heartlands of traditional EU primacy: many in Brussels were taken aback when China created a formal secretariat for its new Central and Eastern European initiative, along with a new credit line for projects in these countries. EU policymakers express frustration that overall figures on Chinese financial support have not been available, in part due to Beijing's opacity, but in part because member states have struck bilateral deals themselves without sharing information with their European partners.

The EU arms embargo has not been lifted, but member states implement it to highly differing degrees, especially in relation to civilian goods and technologies that can also have military uses (although overall military transfers to China remain comparatively low). Under Nicolas Sarkozy's presidency, France made the most abrupt turn from an outspoken line on Tibetan independence to dropping all talk of the Dalai Lama as it led the charge to have China invest in the European stability fund. One harsh judgment is that, "in putting short-term need above long-term vision, Europe risks reducing its supposedly strategic partnership with Beijing to a profit-making opportunity—for China."[35] Moderate pro-Europeans within the Chinese leadership are offset by a nationalist strand of elite opinion that argues that Europe should be "taught a lesson" while it is weak.

Trade has become increasingly competitive rather than complementary as China moves up the value chain. Any decrease in the trade deficit during the crisis stems more from lower European demand than a long-term rebalancing of economic relations with China. Access restrictions on European investors have actually increased since China's accession to the WTO in 2002. Though negotiations have been running since 2007, the EU has gained little ground in its efforts to persuade China to sign a new cooperation agreement that would oblige Beijing to accept fewer preferences as a developing state. Without a Partnership and Cooperation Agreement, a bilateral free trade agreement is not on the agenda. Existing bilateral investment treaties with China have failed to pry open the Chinese market. China wants a new EU-level investment treaty to offer better investment protection but not offer more open access to the Chinese market; indeed, it has complained that a reversal of new market restrictions in several EU member states is a prerequisite to engaging in serious talks.[36] The EU Chamber of Commerce in China bemoans the fact that market access has become more difficult as reforms have atrophied and state-owned enterprise vested interests block further openings. Leading businesses argue that it is now difficult to gain any huge increase in investment opportunities without deeper changes in governance structures; they see European governments as being increasingly impotent to correct these problems. Investor representatives lament that the relatively healthy European private sector has been dragged down by formal EU-China relations now focused so heavily on the debt crisis. They judge the EU-China Strategic Partnership to be "invisible" for businesses. Even the European Chamber of Commerce says it achieves more by lobbying the U.S. embassy than the EU, such is the loss of the union's influence.

INTERDEPENDENT BALANCE

These trends are clearly ominous from a European perspective. However, relations with Asia are not only about creeping subordination; in many respects they have come to be conditioned rather by a more balanced, mutual shaping. Asian states quickly realized they would be hit hard by the eurozone's collapse. The initial 2008 banking crisis made Asian states more nervous about their high degree of dependence on the United States and thus more desirous of rapprochement with European countries. As the broader eurozone crisis deepened, they became concerned over the impact of European banks deleveraging their exposure in Asia. Mainly as a result of the euro crisis, between 2010 and 2012 net private capital flows to emerging Asia virtually halved.[37] The Overseas Development Institute highlights that the Asia-Pacific is more vulnerable than any other region to the retraction in European bank lending. While bank lending to Asia recovered from a dramatic fall in 2009, it began to decrease again from mid-2011; at this stage, Asia was still the most highly leveraged region to European bank credits. Asia was set to be the region that suffered the largest output losses attributable to the crisis, with Bangladesh, Sri Lanka, Vietnam, Cambodia, Indonesia, and the Philippines highly vulnerable to slackening demand for exports to Europe.[38] Most of Asia remains keen on having the euro as a counterbalance reserve currency to the dollar and concerned at how the currency's plight rebounds unfavorably on its own long-term objectives.[39] Some economists insist that Europe's worry is not so much Asia's relative strengths but the prospect of its economic miracle grinding to a postcrisis halt.[40]

One Chinese official summarizes the mutually entwining impact of the crisis: "Your interest is our interest." Some observers suggest that China has not posited the change of dynamics in terms of its "ruling" over Europe but rather as a signal that Chinese investment in Europe is more vital to maintain the Communist Party's model of domestic growth and stability.[41] China still sees shoring up the euro to counterbalance the dollar as in its interest, even as it contemplates the renminbi's broader role. It has helped prop up the value of the embattled euro in part to keep the renminbi down and protect its export competitiveness. For all of China's protestations about European currency imperialism, it has been keen to prevent the euro from falling in value and undercutting its own export strategy.[42] While figures are murky and contested, one economist estimates that China went from holding 26 percent of its reserves in euros in 2010 to 30 percent by the start of 2013.[43] The China Investment Corporation created a $30 billion fund specifically for investment opportunities in the EU.

Ironically, China's desire to pry itself away from "Chimerica" means the regime has begun to look more favorably at investments in Europe and needs Europe more than before the crisis. The significant shift for global economics will be the Chinese turn toward stimulating domestic demand and away from an export-driven model. Some writers insist that China already exhibits rampant consumer demand, rendering it all the more deeply affected by the Western crises.[44] The EU's hope is that China will need to import more from Europe, even if Chinese officials see the new model as being more about the consumption of internal production. The scenario opens the door for growth-based cooperation. One of China's most respected EU experts, Chen Zhimin, points out that China's frustration is now with Europe's weakness and inability to follow a single policy, rather than with any weight member states might have had in pressing particular political differences with Beijing.[45] He argues that before the crisis, EU-China relations were becoming more fractious, but that as a result of the crisis China has actually become more cooperative; this is linked to the gravity of the crisis for China's own interests. Paradoxically the feeling in Beijing is that the power balance of the relationship is now "very much reversed," and this has imbued the Chinese with a sense of responsibility for helping to contain the euro crisis.[46]

The crisis has not entirely reversed the overall commercial asymmetry that remains in Europe's favor. The EU is one of the top two or three trading partners for nearly all Asian states; in contrast, most Asian states are well down the rankings of the EU's top trading partners. As of 2012, the EU accounted for around 10 per cent of ASEAN's trade, whereas ASEAN accounted for only 5 percent of the EU's trade.[47] With markets calmer, more optimistic European officials insist they have begun to feel less supine dependency on Asia.

The EU still matters to India. Some Indians blame the euro crisis for the dip in their own growth rate; ironically, this is the reason for their reluctance to open up trade to the EU. The problem is not so much Indian strength but abiding weaknesses that have held it back from opening up to the EU, especially in services and intellectual property rights. India still exports more to the EU than to the United States and China combined. Talks have dragged, but India has remained engaged in what could be the world's more ambitious trade liberalization accord. One report shows that slow-growing Japan has worried most about the loss of export earnings due to the eurozone crisis, while India has despaired most at the loss of a European geopolitical counterweight to the United States and China.[48]

Moreover, EU policies have not been entirely supine. The EU can be said to have proceeded through three stages in its trade policy with China: a period of cooperative engagement based on technical capacity building to help China meet WTO commitments; when disputes began to emerge more often, an increasing recourse to the WTO dispute mechanisms; and what is now a more adversarial stance of threatening unilateral tit-for-tat bargaining.[49] Two European commissioners proposed subjecting Chinese investments in Europe to a security probe. It is significant that this has not led to any concrete policy measures and that the overall number of EU actions against China has not begun to rise notably. Yet, some politicians still anticipate and advocate future moves in this direction.

Member states agree that the EU-U.S. free trade area now being negotiated is geopolitical: a means of dealing with China. China's quid pro quo—

albeit, not explicitly stated—for direct assistance to the bailout fund was that the EU lift the arms embargo and grant market economy status; the EU did not budge on either of these demands. Pressure from European firms won out—market economy status would make it harder to impose antidumping duties on China. Three-quarters of countries have already given China such status, which it gets automatically in 2016.

All Chinese interlocutors in Beijing speak with concern about how the European Commission's assertive line on trade may abort China's more positive interest in partnership. One expert observes that EU toughness is such as to have ramped up a "dirty trade war" that has rendered the High-Level Economic and Trade Dialogue entirely "dysfunctional."[50] While businesses have pushed the commission to adopt a tougher line toward China, they also now fret about retaliation. European Chamber of Commerce representatives in China even fear that the tone of EU policy has become too adversarial. The previous chapter outlined how in 2013 the commission threatened legal action against China for trade distortions in the solar panel and telecommunications sectors, before using this as leverage to seek negotiated accords with Beijing.

A POLITICAL PARTNERSHIP?

One of the liveliest debates in EU circles has been over whether the union should seek to define a security role in Asia. Some say this represents one of the EU's most urgent, yet-ungrasped strategic imperatives. Others argue it is a fanciful notion, beyond Europe's capacities and outside its circle of vital interests. Skeptics argue that a postcrisis EU cannot seriously hope to exert political-security influence in Asia and that it should not be thus diverted by a fashionable chimera from what are its genuinely pressing, closer-to-home interests. They ridicule the EU's concern with maritime tensions in Asia as confused and unfounded: China is unlikely to cut off export routes upon which it depends more than anyone else; there is little scope for cooperative security approaches of the kind that the EU preaches; and the real risk to European interests would be to invoke Beijing's ire by emboldening smaller Asian states against China. From the hyper-realist perspective, the EU can at most have an impact in an indirect way, by assuming clearer leadership in its own neighborhood in order to free up U.S. capabilities in

Asia. Skeptics allege that the perception is widespread in Asia that the EU has little relevance in the area of security.[51]

Cautious EU policies certainly exhibit some implicit sympathy with these skeptical arguments. Nonetheless, the EU has gingerly taken steps to fashion a more political partnership with and presence in Asia. In 2012 Catherine Ashton for the first time attended the ASEAN Regional Forum. The EU upgraded its East Asia policy guidelines to emphasize geopolitical commitments.[52] In mid-2012, the U.S. State Department approached the EU for deeper cooperation in the South China Sea and even pressed European governments to ramp up their military presence in Asia. Ashton and Hillary Clinton launched a more regular and structured transatlantic dialogue on Asian security. They committed to cooperating on maritime security and trade reciprocity in particular. Ashton attended the Shangri-La Dialogue for the first time in June 2013 and stated that this denoted a strong EU commitment to being a security partner for the region, based on its "innovate, comprehensive approach . . . not projecting power, but empowering."[53]

EU diplomats insist they now build in a far stronger link between economic and political interests, for example in how arms sales must factor in likely power balances: the fact that the EU has an arms embargo on China but has increased arms sales to other Asian countries itself entails geopolitical consequences. The UK carried out naval exercises in the South China Sea in 2011; other military-to-military contacts have intensified. The UK also signed a new defense and security cooperation agreement with Japan in July 2013. France sees itself as having pushed to persuade other member states to add a security component to Europe's Asian policies.[54] Governments have hinted at a broader strategic partnership. Then German Foreign Minister Guido Westerwelle insisted that Asia should be pushed to assume a "greater share of responsibility for the world."[55] Italy's new Asia strategy states that "Asia was once the land of new markets—already it is the land of new partners."[56]

In October 2011 Catherine Ashton met with Chinese defense minister Liang Guanglie and agreed to explore possible military cooperation in the area of maritime patrols. After the third EU-China Strategic Dialogue in July 2012, the two sides planned to engage in deeper cooperation in crisis management, counter-piracy, and maritime security; to hold a regular dialogue on defense and security policy; and to increase training exchanges. Ashton hinted that a lifting of the arms embargo might indirectly be connected to Chinese cooperation on regional security issues. Participants reveal that the Strategic Dialogue has moved onto systematic efforts at coordination on policies in areas such as Africa and Latin America, as well as incorporating security policy personnel from both sides. It has thickened into a multiple-layered set of consultations among diplomats, country special representatives, regional ambassadors, and conflict management units. In 2013, the EU and China agreed to hold a high-level conference on security and defense cooperation. By 2013, there seemed to be scope for cooperation with China over North Korea, as Beijing clearly tired of Pyongyang's provocations.

South Korea in particular seeks a broader partnership with the EU, as it feels squeezed between China, Japan, and the United States. Diplomats in Seoul report that cooperation has begun on human rights support, climate change, development policy, the Middle East, and crisis management. They also insist that while South Korea has sometimes criticized the provision of European humanitarian aid to the North, it has come to see European engagement with Pyongyang as offering a useful conduit. As the new Park administration has tilted more toward engagement with North Korea, diplomats in Seoul report that dialogue with the EU on this issue has been revived.

In addition, the EU-Japan free trade area will be accompanied by a parallel, upgraded political agreement. Senior diplomats also emphasize that priority effort has been exerted to make the EU-India strategic partnership more political. Bilaterally, France and the UK have deepened nuclear cooperation deals with India. In addition, counter-radicalization cooperation has deepened appreciably in several places, especially Pakistan. The EU-Pakistan five-year Engagement Plan was also explicitly framed to go beyond economic issues to include security matters.

One of the most senior EAS diplomats defines the aim as reinforcing the EU's identity as a "principled champion of rules-based, cooperative security." Events in 2012 and 2013 have deepened the view that Asia's economic integration increasingly stands at odds with its rising political nationalism and zero-sum geopolitical rivalries, warranting a more geostrategic European response. The EU has moved further to upgrade existing, low-profile programs on border management, maritime patrols, and training in preventive diplomacy with Japan and ASEAN.[57] Indeed, in 2013 the EAS launched an initiative on maritime security under the rubric of EU-ASEAN relations to support a code of conduct and broader regional rules. As the United States has not ratified the UN Convention on the Law of the Sea, it is less well placed for such rules-based mediation in Asia. A new framework for security dialogue that commenced under the East Asia summit rubric in late 2013 offers a potential access point for the EU to share experiences in the development of a rules-based security community.

Despite the laudable and measured new commitments, much doubt persists that Europe's security turn to Asia amounts to anything substantial. One of the most seasoned EU-Asia watchers laments that "Europeans remain stuck in the one-dimensional vision of Asia's rise being purely about economic opportunities."[58] European defense cuts mean that the EU cannot realistically be relevant in terms of military capacities in Asia. Even France and the UK have reduced their military assets in Asia to a minimum. Despite upgrading military cooperation, member states share little information with each other. Europe is not of strong, direct relevance in supporting the U.S. pivot. An ASEAN Charter was ratified in 2008, just as Europe was descending into crisis; this reenergized the organization but still around the principle of nonintervention. In an effort to boost engagement, the EU has largely aligned itself with this long-standing Asian norm. Yeo Lay Hwee argues that the EU's relevance as a security actor is impeded by a continuing unwillingness in the region to contemplate non-realist concepts of security.[59] Notwithstanding a number of modest crisis management and mediation initiatives in Southeast Asia, the EU's profile has remained that of a developmental humanitarian and not a security actor.[60] The EU has put negligible effort into cooperating on deeper multilateralism with South Korea, which has been keen to contribute to making international institutions more effective.

Once again, a reversal of long-standing power dynamics has become faintly perceptible. European diplomats feel that just as they have offered greater political engagement, Asian states have cooled to the idea: while the latter have long pushed for EU involvement as a counterweight to China, at the same time they have become more nervous about angering Beijing. China has effectively prevented outside involvement aimed at cooperative security in the region. The EU has insisted on Partnership and Cooperation Agreements to accompany free trade agreements as a platform for broader political engagement, but this has been in the face of reluctance from some states to accept it as a foreign policy actor. European officials feel that the EU has responded to Asian complaints over its narrow economic focus only to be rebuffed by the same states previously calling for a more strategic engagement. As a result, EU political involvement has remained limited to extremely low-key initiatives on such issues as nuclear safety and border management. Singapore has blocked the EU's guest participation in the East Asia Summit.

Much debate has been dominated by the U.S. "rebalance," widely judged to be one of the most meaningful geostrategic shifts in recent years. The United States has committed to moving military assets from Europe to Asia and to building up military cooperation with nearly all Asian states except China, even signing a defense cooperation agreement with Vietnam's communist regime. The EU has finely balanced its response. Many in the EU express ambivalence over the pivot and do not want the EU to be too associated with its implied message that the overriding security challenge is to contain China militarily. The European argument is that more positive security engagement with China makes the EU useful by virtue of "not being the United States"; rather than undermining Washington's pivot, diplomats claim the union delivers something useful to its ally. Officials ponder whether the new U.S. approach signals a divergence of transatlantic views on Asia. China expressed unease over the Clinton-Ashton commitment to a new EU-U.S. Dialogue on Asian security. Senior German officials opine that the pivot's main implication for Europe is that it obliges the EU to deal more independently with its own neighborhood, an indirect impact being more significant than any direct bearing on Europe's own Asia policy.

Jonas Parello-Plesner welcomes the EU's reluctance fully to align with the U.S. pivot. In his view, the EU is strong in designing comprehensive strategies for nontraditional risks, which is what Asian security will most acutely be concerned with; it has also been wise to keep its trade deals less politicized than the Trans-Pacific Partnership, which in expressly excluding China is now widely perceived to be part of a U.S. strategy to contain China.[61] While the United States has come to support regional integration more strongly and rejects criticism that its approach is aimed against China, it is widely accused of straining Asian unity by pressing states to be aligned with U.S. containment of China. The EU line, meanwhile, is that security depends on stronger regional integration. The danger is seen to reside in a combination of the Chinese Communist Party's internal insecurity and its external overconfidence. The many disputes over contested islands have been seen as important primarily for the process through which they are addressed; the EU has sought to nudge the U.S. pivot toward a focus on economic cooperation and inclusive security. However, while the EU says it wants maritime disputes to be resolved through the rule of law, it has little in the way of concrete instruments to back up this call. In conversation, many European diplomats still express a strikingly modest degree of ambition on Asia, welcoming the enhancement of U.S. engagement as relieving the EU of having to worry about an Asian security strategy in the midst of financial meltdown. In an informal Quint process, some of the larger member states express more geopolitical empathy with the United States than is conveyed in many EU-level statements.

Other limits persist, too. Diplomats acknowledge that the EU still struggles to make direct linkages and trade-offs between economic and political aspects in the same way that the United States does. The EU rarely seems to consider how its economic policies affect geopolitical interests. Some in the region complain that as the big powers tempt individual Asian states with bilateral trade deals, this stirs political rivalries within the region. One Asian ambassador complains that the EU is "just trying to get things out of Asia, not thinking how we can really cooperate. . . . After thirty-five years of dialogue with ASEAN, the EU shows no real urgency in talking in broader political terms with the region." Japan in particular has stressed that European governments still need to engage politically and move beyond their tendency to relegate Asia to one giant "business opportunity."[62] One senior Japanese view is that the erstwhile "indifferent" and "neutral" EU has begun to realize the impact of Asian security on European interests because of changing economic power balances, but it still tends to reduce "strategic interests" to very direct economic impacts.[63] Japanese diplomats still do not see the EU as having any significant complement to its dependence on the United States for security cover. One close observer points out that, despite warm mood music, EU-Asia security links remain "practically non-existent."[64] The EU is still absent from nuclear diplomacy on North Korea, as efforts continue to restart some kind of process.

In terms of security relations with China itself, the road to strategic partnership has remained bumpy. The defense dimension to EU-China talks could develop into something genuinely deeper, but so far it has produced nothing tangible. The EU's 50-plus sectoral dialogues with China lack strategic focus. Talking to analysts in China, it is difficult to understate the legacy of distrust that European intervention in Libya has left even among relatively liberal Chinese voices. A revamp of the EU's strategic partnership with China in late 2012 was acknowledged by diplomats to be largely formulaic, bereft of new policy approaches. Member state diplomats in Beijing acknowledge that the political will to engage may have strengthened but that they now grapple with the question of what resources the EU actually has today that count politically. Chinese officials lament in private that the EU still does not think of China as a political power in the same way as the United States does and that if anything, the crisis has compounded Europe's adherence to an economic lens.

While Germany's presence in Beijing is clearly the primary European influence, the country's diplomats tend to see little foreign or security policy role for Europe. Some member state diplomats insist it is difficult to sell the EU as a global partner at the same time that they are asking China to rescue such an acute economic mess. The EU's strategic dialogue with China remains a pale imitation of the U.S. equivalent. Diplomats in Beijing acknowledge that most issues on the agenda of the strategic dialogue remain too sensitive to have produced any tangible results. They report that China sees the strategic dialogue as being a vehicle for influencing European positions on issues such as Syria or Iran, while resisting talk of EU involvement in Asian security.

The EU has eschewed any strong, active stance on the disputed islands that pepper the region. In the summer of 2012 the United States ratcheted up criticism of Chinese actions in the South China Sea, in particular condemning the upgraded Chinese military presence on the Paracel Islands. The United States was widely seen as backing other Asian states' claims against China. The EU has seen itself as being more neutral. Even as tensions soared frighteningly between China and Japan in autumn 2012, the EU remained unengaged. Insiders reveal that one of the main reasons for EU passivity on the islands dispute was pressure from China not to get involved. For this reason, representatives of other Asian states privately expressed disappointment with the union's apparent willingness to sit on the sidelines. The EU has not maximized what it could be contributing in rule-based mediation to complement the U.S. role.[65]

It remains unclear what the EU would do in the event of a conflagration in the Taiwan Strait. While the current KMT government in Taiwan has reduced cross-strait tensions since 2008, Taiwanese diplomats complain that they have received little reward from European governments—indeed, they stand penalized by the EU-South Korea free trade deal—and that the EU is still overly sanguine about the future strategic risk of mainland Chinese preponderance. Taiwan officials in Taipei feel their pressure for an agreement with the EU has met with a wall of European unresponsiveness, despite the willingness to label an accord merely as an Economic and Cooperation Agreement in deference to Chinese sensitivities. They complain that member states have de facto circumvented the restrictions of the arms embargo on China. They would like to see EU support on maritime patrols. They have also ratcheted up pressure on the EU to support Taiwanese entry into the Asia-Europe Meeting, as well as other international bodies. On all these petitions, the feeling among interlocutors in Taipei is that the economic crisis has significantly reinforced Europe's reticence to do anything at all that could be uncomfortable for Beijing. The criticism among Taiwanese diplomats is that the EU believes that now that Taiwan is not actively confronting China, it needs less support; in fact, they argue, it needs external support to maintain the policy of rapprochement without endangering Taiwan's de facto independence.

One Pakistani ambassador argues that as the EU's main contribution to security affairs, it needs to try harder to be a bridge between Pakistan and the United States. Specifically, the EU can no longer merely offer useful development assistance and trade incentives but shirk the tough security matters, refusing to talk about Kashmir at India's behest and quitting Afghanistan while leaving little behind in terms of necessary strategic presence. On the other side of the divide, Indian experts feel that the EU is beginning to realize that it has a stake in Asian security challenges but still underestimates the potential for conflict and instability in the region. Indians are moderately content that the EU is beginning to see their point on state-sponsored terrorism even if they still think the EU is too soft and developmental in its approach to Pakistan. They press for EU cooperation on state strengthening in Pakistan to deal with radicalism. New Delhi has also sought cooperation on the "Indian Ocean power highway" and on "dealing with China." Advice and incentives for a healthier "triangulation" of relations with China and India are often mentioned as a potential future role for the EU, moving beyond a tendency to treat the two great rising powers of Asia in zero-sum isolation from each other.

CONCLUSION

The economic crisis has given a belated but exciting new jolt to Europe's relations with rising Asia. Many sober observers point out that this rapprochement still has a long road to travel to produce tangible, significant, and lasting policy output. Yet, the evolution of Asia policy undoubtedly constitutes one of the most dramatic changes to EU foreign policy in recent years. It is ironic that it took such a profound crisis fully to awaken Europe to Asia's importance—although this is in line with the reactive, needs-driven dynamic that habitually predominates in EU external strategy. Indeed, the paradox is that the EU has moved to court Asia just as the power balance between the two regions appears to have taken another decisive lurch eastward. The discourse has somewhat broadened: not only is the focus now on "what is the EU role in Asia?" but also "what is the Asian role in Europe?"—although while economic relations have become more balanced, the security dialogue still has a one-way focus on whether the EU has any role in Asia, much less on engaging with Asia's broader international role. The crisis has left Europe more solicitous of—but also more beholden to—Asian powers, and China in particular. However, there are good reasons to hope that the crisis will breed a realization of deeply entwined interdependence rather than competition for relative gain between the two regions. Assertive commercial posturing on both sides will need to abate for this positive scenario to take root.

It is said that the U.S. strategy in Asia has become "engage and hedge." The EU's might be described as "narrower engagement, with slightly less anxious hedging." The EU has set realistic boundaries to its political pretensions in Asia. However, despite the progress made, it could be doing more both to safeguard its own strategic interests and to prompt Asian powers in the direction of rules-based cooperative security. There is demand in

Asia—even if inconsistently followed through—for a more political partnership with Europe. Despite the broadening out of EU-Asian relations
since the financial crisis commenced, Asian governments ritually complain
that the union still approaches them only for short-term commercial deals.
The EU will not be a leading security power in Asia, but it at least needs
a clear position and engagement on key strategic issues, and especially on
how its actions relate to the U.S. role in the region.

A modest soft security role is appropriate, and not entirely meaningless.
The EU should pay greater heed to Asian states that want European help
to boost international rules as a means of influencing Chinese behavior;
conversely, it is right to avoid collusive bandwagoning against China. One
extensive research consortium concludes that the EU could play a useful
role as a mediating bridge between the United States and different constellations of Asian powers.[66] The question is not one of the EU directly
undertaking major security operations but of cooperating with Asian states
on shared global challenges. One side effect of the eurozone crisis is that
the EU has begun to get far more serious about a deeper partnership with
Asia. In the aftermath of the crisis, the union will still need to sharpen its
focus in order to strike the right balance between over- and underplaying
its hand in Asia.

CHAPTER 6

GOODBYE, LIBERAL WORLD ORDER?

The long-term impact of the eurozone crisis makes it harder for the EU to retain a focus on normative political values within its foreign policies. Many would say it is largely futile and misplaced for the EU even to try to do so. European capabilities are diminished and, some argue, the liberal world order is in its death throes. EU foreign policy is caught between internal crisis and the rise of non-Western powers. Paraphrasing Horace's reflection after Rome defeated the Greeks, the EU has an uphill task to tame its tamers.

Building from chapter four's look at the travails of economic liberalism, this chapter assesses the EU's postcrisis commitment to the more political dimensions of the liberal world order. One strand of the EU's response reflects a conviction that an enfeebled Europe today has even more incentive to shape the international agenda in favor of liberal values. A converse sentiment has also hardened, however, that the EU must more graciously accept that the core values of the liberal world order are now so besieged so as to make their defense a dissonant and reckless endeavor. The chapter finds that crisis-hit Europe is certainly a less proselytizing force, but that in areas of its foreign policies retains support for liberal values. While the EU is still a liberal power, it is more selectively so. But the challenge of molding geostrategy to a different kind of liberal order remains perilously unmet.

ECLECTIC WORLD ORDER(S)

A legion of experts declares the demise of the liberal world order. It has become commonplace to assert that a zero-sum logic has returned to dominate international politics. What is termed "rise and fall realism" sees periods of adjustment to global power as being those least amenable to shared values and most susceptible to conflict. A by-product of the financial crisis is that the critique of economic liberalism increasingly spills over into a doubting of the creed's political dimensions. The crisis places the focus of attention back on self-interested state behavior, with relative gains against other nations sought above multilateral rules.[1] It has been interpreted as another step away from the original hopes of a politically driven liberal governance of global institutions—a trend that was already under way thanks to the subordination of political to economic interests, and the distortion of liberal interventionism by Western security interests.[2]

Ian Bremmer argues that the world is set for an uneasy interregnum between the U.S.-run liberal order and a still-pending new order; this indeterminate state will necessarily be characterized by fierce self-help state strategies.[3] Mark Leonard judges that "rather than being transformed by their membership of the [international] institutions, the rising powers are dramatically changing the nature of the institutions themselves."[4] Charles Kupchan opines that the West's norms have little global appeal and that as its material dominance wanes, it will not be able to browbeat others to accept them. Interdependence will magnify tensions, not temper them. It is impossible that power can shift without norms mutating, too. China has not challenged the liberal order more fully only because it is not yet strong enough to do so. In this line of reasoning, the West must attach less priority to global multilateral rules and accept that problems will be managed by regional organizations without outside interference.[5] Martin Jacques insists that a powerful China will bring with it a sure-footed economic diplomacy that others will be obliged to adopt and a completely different type of universalism based on "harmonious and humane authority."[6] Some writers believe that in practice the liberal order has only ever taken root in a very limited manner anyway, making its slide toward irrelevance even more inevitable and the need for more limited and pragmatic alliances more natural.[7] Others insist that climate change is an additional and potentially defining factor pushing against liberal interdependence and toward more zero-sum realpolitik.[8]

The most prominent strand of academic opinion has been in favor of "thinner" forms of universalism.[9] Progressives now commonly argue that liberal multilateralism should give way to a genuine competition over new ideas for international order.[10] Prominent experts conclude that trends disadvantage democracy's fortunes and that authoritarian resilience is a more powerful countertrend.[11]

Defending the opposing argument, John Ikenberry has for many years insisted that rising powers do not threaten the liberal world order so much as they want more of a say in running it. Institutions are thicker now than in the past, making China's rise qualitatively different; China may overtake the United States economically, but overturning a whole world order is a different matter. We confuse the loss of Western hegemony with the demise of liberalism, because these two things have historically gone hand in hand. Other powers do not object to the liberal world order per se so much as the West's failure to respect its ostensible rules. "Western order" and "liberal order" are no longer synonymous.[12] The deepening of cooperation across many areas of policy invalidates the classic theory that as one set of powers falls and another rises, conflict over fundamental values is inevitable. "Defensive structural realism" reads from history the lesson that rising powers have been cautious about disturbing a status quo, as structural conditions mean their interests are unlikely to be served by aggressive challenges to prevailing dynamics.

Many experts argue that it is unduly simplistic to posit a world returning to old-style statist multipolarity. As power drifts from Western states to Eastern states, in overall terms it also drifts away from states per se. State power itself is more evanescent and more restricted in the latitude it affords governments; power is shared more widely but in a form that stymies decisions and spreads irreverence.[13] The new order is more polycentric, drawing dynamism from increased social empowerment and interconnections.[14] While a "resurgent south" has rejected the more simplistic tenets of the Washington consensus, its rise has been driven by a spectacular thickening of economic, political, social, educational, civil society, and technological interconnectedness among emerging states themselves.[15] Rising powers have signed up to more international treaties and norms than has the United

States. De-bordering advances. Empathetic, global "we-feeling" belies the brute inhumanity between societies that suffused previous periods of history. The future will be one of multi-stakeholder hubs, with governments playing a coordinating role over networks rather than exerting zero-sum, hierarchical monopoly of influence. Even cheerleaders for Asia's assertive rise speak of a "great convergence" around the norms of reason and law across different regions of the world.[16]

The London School of Economics's noted annual survey of global civil society has recorded a gradual thickening and reenergizing of transborder civic linkages into 2013.[17] David Held sees the gradual emergence of "layered cosmopolitanism," with rights attaching to global citizens rather than nations.[18] Philip Cerny proposes a framework of "transnational neopluralism" to capture the growing density of cross-border networks at all levels: international relations is giving way to world politics.[19] Ulrich Beck has famously posited a "realistic cosmopolitanism" that goes with the flow of the world's already-existing "cosmopolitan outlook" rather than trying, Canute-like, to resist it.[20] A step further, Niall Ferguson has, controversially, argued that the "others" have caught up because they now have greater faith in what were assumed to be Western values than many in the West itself.[21] It has similarly been argued that the underlying problem is Europe's apathy over liberal values, not a fundamental drift to a different model of international policy economy at the global level.[22]

It is probably most convincing to conceive the emerging global order as an eclectic mix of these two positions. The most compelling accounts of the emerging global order point to the variety of trends that now condition the structure of international politics. The liberal world order stands neither gloriously unscathed nor mortally wounded. Politically, Western states have never fully adhered to the principles of a liberal world order in practice anyway: there is thus no dramatic rupture. The challenge of matching rhetoric to reality has long existed and continues. The liberal world order faced this challenge yesterday, faces it today, and will face it tomorrow. There is no shift from white to black but between shades of gray. There is no pristine, fixed liberal world order that socializes passive "others"; rather, there are mutually negotiated rules that evolve in contrasting directions. Liberal norms are neither immutable nor entirely repellent to rising powers. Rather than a singular, uni-directional trend deepening or weakening liberal order, movements may rather resemble a pendulum swinging between internationalism and isolationism as citizens tend to blame whichever of these conditions prevails at any given moment. What is taking shape, perhaps, is a hybrid order that needs disaggregating and understanding in its component parts.

Liberal values are simultaneously more widely attacked *and* more broadly supported. Analysts disagree on some fundamentals: how far the liberal order can be reformed from core post-1945 forms without losing its essential spirit; how dependent this order is on American power; whether it is essentially a hegemonic or benign-universalist project; over the extent to which non-Western powers support basic liberal principles; and hence whether incipient changes to this order are in form or content.[23] From a critical perspective it is argued that Western power interests have always underlain the liberal order and that the demise of American hegemony opens the way to a benign rethink—even if this means questioning some of the rights, laws, and rules usually seen as necessarily forming the core of a liberal order.[24]

Different dynamics are likely to prevail across different policy areas. China has a nuanced position: it is highly dissatisfied with aspects of the liberal world order, but it seeks merely incremental and partial change rather than a rupture to a completely different type of ordering principle.[25] Chinese interlocutors are adamant that they do not seek the universalization of any illiberal Chinese model, which is based on the very judgment that political values are contingent. China has begun to buy into some elements of global economic governance, but it resists being shackled by rules on security as it seeks to stake its dominance in Asia. Russia has a stake in various international security forums, but with its energy-driven geoeconomics is reluctant to be bound by international economic rules.[26] Rising democracies resist many elements of Western democracy promotion, but it is not true that they are entirely realist in their thinking; indeed, some elements of their external policies now genuinely seek to support liberal political reform in other states.[27] Prominent theorists highlight that this is not an "either/or" question: many aspects of the liberal order have depended on non-Western powers and not solely on the United States steering global politics; their rise militates in favor of aspects of that core order but also suggests that very different paths to modernity will be reflected in its evolution.[28]

GATE-KEEPING MULTILATERALISM

In the past five years these difficult-to-read trends have fused with the constraints of the eurozone crisis to effect a joint external and internal impact on EU foreign policy. If incertitude prevails analytically, the practical evolution of EU foreign policy has also hovered between commitment to and doubt over the liberal world order. While general support for multilateral values has been relatively resilient to the crisis, it is not the undisputed driving force of a European geostrategic vision. European governments increasingly judge how much space is left over for multilateral principles from strategic calculations rather than seeing such values as integral to the latter. No European policymaker will say that the EU has abandoned multilateral values; but they will almost without exception muse that to push internationalist values today goes against the grain. The sentiment is that the EU cannot do much to nudge global politics in this direction and that this therefore makes for more complicated geostrategy.

European support for multilateralism persists but has also wavered. One particularly authoritative expert detects a new "normative uncertainty" in the EU's inelegant admixture of "bi-multilateralism" that has clouded the advancement of "negotiated order."[29] European governments today support multilateralism not so much as an overriding and structural organizing principle of international relations, but as an instrumental tool: they shop for diverse groupings of states that are seen as tangibly useful for negotiating deals and trade-offs, as a means to maximize relative gain, not to embed a particular shape to global order. One EU research project concludes that while the union retains the goal of more formalized and organized global-level multilateralism, in practice it has recently shifted toward a more ad hoc form of multilateralism, varying across issues and with select and varied clusters of partners.[30] Experts still distinguish Europe's institutionalist understanding of multilateralism—the process of consultation as an end in itself that helps mold cooperative positions—from the U.S. tendency to assess multilateral bodies in a more results-oriented, problem-solving manner. But they also observe that the EU has itself gradually moved to a more critical questioning of and more contingent support for multilateralism.[31]

The EU has been driven toward a preference for minilateral groupings in security questions by the structure of the changing order; power balances are in flux, agendas are still being shaped, and thus stable multilateral coalitions for security matters are difficult to form.[32] One study finds little evidence of the EU using its bilateral strategic partnerships to lever multi-lateral cooperation on the financial crisis.[33]

By late 2013, the momentum in the G20 behind globally designed regulatory norms had clearly abated, in part because of rising powers' resistance and in part due to European governments' almost exclusive concern with internal EU debates over supervisory rules connected to prospective banking union. European states have used the G20 more for direct support of their own economic problems than for pushing deeply rooted multi-lateral solutions. Germany and France have not agreed on reforms to the international monetary system or the desirability of active intervention to manage the euro exchange rate. Internal EU cooperation has not necessarily presaged multilateral coordination: while efforts to move EU rules up to the multilateral level can often still guide a way to overcoming barriers to collective action, conversely they can sometimes rub against the emergence of more "co-shaped" and legitimate global norms.

The trend of the various functional Gs is toward "executive-led multi-lateralism."[34] The crisis has forced European governments to look at global institutions less in terms of "the value of rules" and more as potential sources of tangible support: China's development banks lend far more to poor states today than does the IMF, which now lends mainly to Europe. Chinese interlocutors complain that a G2 would submit China to the tutelage of U.S. demands and thus express disappointment at the paucity of European efforts to engage with Beijing on a remodeled multilateralism. They see European governments as having lost interest in using the G20 to promote reform of the global monetary system, instead focusing merely on pushing for short-term help for European economies through this body. And the same tensions infuse trade policy: the EU has begun to act more assertively against other powers' disregard for multilateral trade rules, while itself more regularly pushing at the boundaries of such rules.

EU officials confirm that the commitment to standard multilateral norms has weakened, and that the focus has moved from multilateralism to a new buzz concept of "flexi-lateralism." The EU has fashioned a more modular approach to international partnerships, in preference to a holistic multilateralism as uniform principle. This is some distance from the seminal definition of true multilateralism as being predicated on the principle of diffused reciprocity.[35]

Despite its identity as "the good multilateral," the EU has not been supportive of the many proposals forwarded to make global institutions less statist and more participative. European states have generally sought to protect multilateral rules but have not been receptive to ideas for the inclusion of transnational networks and cosmopolitan civil society; for strong parliamentary assemblies to exert effective scrutiny at the United Nations and other bodies; for social forums charged with ensuring that governments meet their promises to protect citizens around the world from genocide and serious human rights abuses; for citizens' ombudsmen to monitor the social effects of bodies like the WTO; or for opening up the International Court of Justice to cases brought by citizens rather than states.[36] Nor have they supported more specific, crisis-generated calls for strengthened civic watchdogs of global financial bodies as a means of averting further mismanagement of the banking sector.[37] Multilateral bodies still rest in part on Westphalian principles that serve to underpin nation-states (which is why rising powers hold relatively status quo views on their role).

Overall European funds to multilateral bodies have begun to decrease since 2011.[38] Most member states have been lukewarm toward cooperation on global human rights with new democracies, for fear this would cut across Russia and China. They have put the brakes on ideas pushed by the United States at various stages for a new club of democracies setting strategic guidelines for global affairs. Member state allocations to the United Nations Democracy Fund have decreased. Italy, France, and Spain have pulled out, in direct contradiction to their rhetorical protestation about democracy support needing to be multilateralized; meanwhile, India has pumped up its support for this admirable multilateral initiative.

The subtle change in perspective generated by the crisis emerges in informal conversations with diplomats. One member state official admits: "We know part of the new order is a strand of personal empowerment, but we do not know how to harness this operationally as well as the zero-sum elements." One senior member state planner suggests the EU still needs to forge more "system-shaping" relations with rising powers. Policymakers tend to define a deepening of multilateralism in terms of increasing overall levels of cooperation on specific goals within international institutions, not reassessing the qualitative basis of that cooperation. General comments from officials still equate defending multilateralism with defending European quotas in multilateral bodies, to prevent the increased weight of what they see as more realist powers. Diplomats commonly insist that the general lesson of the past five years, including key failures like the Copenhagen climate summit, is that the EU needs to bargain harder before it makes its own commitments to multilateral solutions rather than approaching the latter as good in and of themselves. The insistence on having another European head of the IMF was not only derided in other regions as subversive of the West's supposed commitment to fairer multilateralism, but it also looked like a dubious case of self-interested nepotism given that the main recipients of IMF funds in the short term were likely to be European states.

SECURITY AND LIBERAL ORDER

The EU's contribution to multilateral military projection for liberal ends seems to have peaked. The weakest point of EU security policy has been its vagueness over how to retain ostensibly core tenets while adapting geostrategically to rising non-Western military power.[39]

Spending on external military deployments has plummeted but risen on internal surveillance within Europe itself, revealing the containment-oriented reordering of priorities. The Common Security and Defense Policy has lost ambition. Officials talk of a new activism in CSDP, with missions in Somalia, Niger, and now Mali. Antipiracy operations off the Horn of Africa have been complemented by rule of law efforts in Somalia, indicating a link between CSDP and political reform aims. The crisis has certainly not congealed CSDP quite as much as many feared. Yet, all these recent missions are in truth rather modest training initiatives for security personnel—useful and important but not evidence of a willingness to engage significantly in conflict resolution.

No pioneers have stepped forward to advance the flexible cooperation foreseen in the Lisbon Treaty. The high profile, in-house review of the External Action Service published in July 2013 acknowledged that, despite an increased number of interagency coordination meetings, the EU has yet to integrate its standard foreign policy instruments into its crisis response mechanisms in a way that makes its vaunted "Comprehensive approach" a reality.[40] Insiders and observers commonly bemoan how CSDP flunked the Libya crisis, which represented exactly the kind of challenge for which it was designed, and has thus lost much credibility with the United States.

French engagements in Côte d'Ivoire, Libya, and Mali denoted a much-remarked new activism. At the same time, these interventions were predicated on tightly delineated rules of engagement and did not transition smoothly into large-scale peace support and democracy-building efforts. In Mali, French military intervention was admirable but also highlighted others' reluctance. Political pressure was also extremely belated on the military, which had intervened twice to replace the government, to expedite a return to the democratic process. Once again, European governments were stuck behind the curve in their patchy efforts to marry security engagements with support for a broader, conflict-tempering political process. Germany was sharply rebuked by Paris for refusing even modest pleas for support in Mali. French troops admirably helped stabilize Mali's internal security but moved to hand over quickly to an African-led mission, and the Hollande government eschewed any deeper conflict resolution engagement. After elections were held in August 2013, the international community seemed content for the Malian army to retain a prominent role. France was so eager to leave that it cut a deal with Touareg groups, which meant that there was no post-election extension of democratic institutions into the north of the country. Indeed, violence returned in November 2013 and two French journalists were killed. This marked a return to the precarious status quo prior to the coup and insurgency.

The preference today is to outsource post-conflict peace building to regional organizations. Germany seems to adhere to a markedly sanguine security policy, which downplays potential geostrategic risks in the world. Spanish troops have been withdrawn from Bosnia and most from Lebanon, too. The case of Syria stands as the most sobering sign of postcrisis European retrenchment. Only France stood ready to intervene militarily in any significant way after the Assad regime's alleged use of chemical weapons in August 2013. A hands-off policy focused on strategic containment of the regional instability that might result from the regime's fall has precluded any notable assistance for Syrian opposition groups. While there have been good grounds for this caution, the lowering of ambition is still striking—as European action has been constricted by a combination of Syrian complexities, internal EU weaknesses, the legacy of Iraq, and skillful Russian diplomacy.

The long-standing Franco-British tandem on hard security issues has in 2012 and 2013 been reduced to a clear French lead, as British doubts have taken root. Critics argue that the UK has forfeited its long-held reputation for excellence in conflict management after two disastrous campaigns in Iraq and Afghanistan. These showed the UK army unable to adjust to local circumstances or to marry military with civilian capacities. The two defeats have left the UK military extremely cautious about further deployments, disoriented in conflict resolution doctrine, and discredited in the eyes of its (especially U.S.) partners.[41] The army will now rely far more on reservists, explicitly so as to help cut the UK's fiscal deficit. General Sir Peter Wall, chief of the general staff, reflected: "The zeitgeist in the post-Afghanistan environment is that we don't want to do one of those again in a hurry … from the army's point of view, we could do with a bit of a break."[42] The British army has moved from a focus on enduring campaigns to preparing for a range of less direct contingencies. It will concentrate instead on training foreign armies better to manage their national security and supporting civil authorities to protect infrastructure at home. Experts observe a switch away from offensive armed forces to homeland security, eviscerating stabilization capabilities beyond the UK's borders.[43] Poland has also pushed for more priority to be attached to territorial defense and less to expeditionary interventionism.[44] Security experts talk of the focus being back on core NATO defense functions and less on "liberal peace-building."

The most serious effect of the eurozone crisis is not so much in the headline figures of defense cuts, but a diminished capability and political will to engage in multilateral peace-protecting missions abroad. The linkage between hard security capacities and the political components of conflict resolution and state-building has ruptured. Of particular note, Ulrich Speck laments an "unbound Pacifism" distorting German views of geopolitics.[45] Italian foreign policy has suffered from a combination of the euro crisis and the country's being shunted from the top table internationally; top Italian experts lament that the country had become utterly "marginalized" within EU security policy.[46] The Spanish Foreign Ministry produced a new security strategy in the autumn of 2012 that was strikingly cautious in its aims and scope.

The process of drawing up a new European Global Strategy, launched in 2012 by Poland, Sweden, Italy, and Spain, has reached an apparent dead end. Other member states have not supported publication of a new, formal strategy. At the end of this process in late 2013, observers noted that the EU still uses such documents to talk of the generic way it prefers to do international relations, not to develop "grand strategy" in the more concrete sense of where and how its power resources are to be deployed with security interests in mind.[47] EAS officials spoke of the need for a series of smaller strategies that were more operationally relevant in different sectors of foreign policy. It was thought that a number of member states would still propose having a new security strategy, but for late 2014 when the new high representative was due to take office. Insiders acknowledged that the focus of the much-heralded defense and security summit in December 2013 would be on cost-saving capability-sharing, not any proactive strategic rethinking.

STILL SUPPORTING DEMOCRACY . . .

For a number of years prior to the eurozone crisis, the EU's support for democratic values around the world was treading water. While many admirable human rights initiatives were pursued and the general commitment to shoring up democracy was retained, European tactics were increasingly equivocal. There was less willingness to react critically to manipulated elections; most country partners won increased European aid and trade preferences even as regimes stole elections. There was an aversion to impose sanctions even in the most repressive states. And the EU prevaricated on the use of enlargement to underwrite democratic advances in Turkey, Ukraine, Moldova, and the Balkans.

In this sense, a period of liberal doubt predated the economic crisis. Since the crisis erupted, it is in some ways surprising how European strategies have become tougher on human rights. The academic community certainly still tends to see the EU's basic strategic vision of the world as distinctive in its strong commitment to liberal notions of security and geopolitics.[48] In some respects, the EU has retained a focus on democracy support more than the United States, Canada, and Japan, all of which have retreated to more cautious positions in recent years. This is in part because the EU has scrambled to respond to increased demand for democratic reform in some countries—a sign that the new world order is not entirely illiberal. It is also due to the fact that this aspect of foreign policy has advanced on an institutional track somewhat disconnected from management of the economic crisis; what might even be seen as an advantage of interagency "incoherence." With so much else going wrong, a modest strengthening of the EU's human rights identity has been seen as helpful compensation.

Pressure for human rights improvements has still been applied. Indeed, the EU appears to have used sanctions more readily. By 2013 the EU had some kind of punitive measure in operation against nearly thirty states. Even though many of these measures were extremely light and targeted, and not related to democracy and human rights, this was by some margin a historical high; indeed, an avalanche of legal cases was open against the EU, alleging that it was overextending itself and penalizing many individuals and companies without due cause.[49] Libya, Syria, and to a lesser extent Iran have been the most prominent cases in this trend. Aid sanctions made a difference in finally pushing Laurent Gbagbo from office in Côte d'Ivoire. In Rwanda, the main European donors, including the European Commission, the Netherlands, and the UK have either frozen or held back aid on human rights grounds. In October 2013 the EU withheld some aid to Bosnia because of reform delays in relation to minority rights. Parcels of aid have been held back from the government in Afghanistan until more far-reaching reform is achieved. The EU has tightened political conditions placed on the large quantities of aid given as direct budget support, reversing a trend after 2000 to deliver more of such funds without governance stipulations. With aid budgets under pressure, governments need to work harder to justify decisions over where development funds are destined.

Europe's biggest funder of democracy and human rights initiatives, Germany, has steadily increased its allocation to government and civil society year on year to more than 1 billion euros ($1.45 billion) in both 2010 and 2011, up from 800 million euros in 2008. In the UK's aid profile, government and civil society is the second-highest category, at 728 million pounds ($1.1 billion) for 2011–2012, behind only the allocation to health. The UK has also begun significantly to increase the share of its governance aid going to civil society rather than governments, as part of a revamped "Capability, Accountability and Responsiveness" framework.[50]

Sweden's funding of its "democracy, human rights, and gender" portfolio has remained relatively constant at just over 400 million euros per year since 2008; this still accounts for 11 percent of overall aid, up from 8 percent before the crisis. In Danish aid, democracy and human rights are defined as the top ranked of only four strategic priorities; in Denmark's new 2011 aid strategy, democracy is accorded absolute pride of place as the pivot around which all other strands of development assistance revolve. Danish democracy and human rights aid has stabilized at roughly 250 million euros a year since 2008; this is now around 20 percent of overall aid, a share that has risen incrementally since the early 2000s.[51] In late 2011 the Dutch Foreign Ministry produced an updated human rights strategy that was couched in strikingly assertive terms; it talked of wielding more sanctions, "holding governments to account" for rights abuses, withdrawing budget support from nondemocratic regimes, and of political criteria guiding the reduction of aid recipients.[52]

The French government presented a new democracy and human rights strategy at the end of 2010 and has embedded "governance units" within its embassies around the world.[53] Central and eastern European states, in particular Poland, the Czech Republic, and Slovakia, have begun to dedicate more funding to democracy projects and have pressed for new democracy initiatives at the EU level; civic organizations from these states have become the most active subcontractors implementing democracy programs funded by other Western and global donors. There remain limits to eastern European commitments, but these states have gradually become more confident players in democracy support.[54]

In 2012 funds from the EU budget allocated for democracy and human rights rose 5.5 percent over the previous year.[55] Despite manifold doubts over its utility, democracy aid has not dried up, but has slowly increased. Taking the myriad EU instruments together, funding levels have held up well. Funding from the European Instrument for Democracy and Human Rights has increased year on year. The conflict-related Instrument for Stability now funds an impressive range of political reform work in crisis states.[56] The European Commission launched a 2.3 billion euro Governance Initiative in 2006 under its mainstream development fund; after several reviews found this to be overly technical, the commission committed to injecting more political reform projects into the initiative. A new policy has also been produced on increasing support to parliaments.[57] Under its Agenda for Action on Democracy Support, the EU in 2012 completed a series of democracy profiles in nine pilot countries to build up a comprehensive map of all European support and internal power dynamics with a view toward more coherent programming post-2014. The European Commission's new Agenda for Change places support for democracy and human rights firmly at the heart of development policy; this support is defined as one of only two strategic priorities in an effort to improve the impact of EU sectoral interventions and link development policy to a more assertive use of political conditionality.[58] A committee has been created in Brussels to introduce political conditions in the use of direct budget support to reduce the risk of its shoring up nondemocratic regimes.

In 2012, a new EU human rights special representative was appointed. This new post was one element of a beefed-up Strategic Framework and Action Plan on Human Rights and Democracy introduced in July 2012. This incorporated a 36-point action plan. Under the action plan, 97 improvements are to be implemented by the end of 2014; by early 2013 nine such steps had been taken, mainly to do with streamlining and strengthening internal EU processes. Human rights strategies have been compiled for nearly 140 states, all with the involvement of civil society. EU delegations and ESDP missions now have human rights and democracy focal points. The EU has put liaison officers into many delegations to help activists under threat. The EIDHR has increased the number of small and flexible grants available for NGO personnel threatened by more restrictive measures, to help pay for security, medical bills, and relocation and legal help. A raft of new projects has commenced on trade unions and labor standards, seen as part of support for deep or social democracy.[59]

In September 2012 the commission published a new strategy on civil society support, promising to intensify backing for democratic activists and for newer, "fluid" forms of social and youth movements, and also to press for more liberal civil society laws.[60] Most visibly, a new European Endowment for Democracy (EED) started work in 2013 with nearly 20 million euros granted by the commission, Poland, Sweden, the Netherlands, and several eastern European member states. The EED defines its approach as bottom-up and aimed at supporting decentralization, unregistered groups and individuals, and online movements that need to link into mainstream political activity.

. . . BUT EVIDENCE IS MIXED

While EU foreign policy has not entirely lost its normative substance, in some ways the crisis seems to have dissuaded European governments from running great risks in defending the liberal world order. Democracy and human rights policy has been only partially salvaged; this area of policy once again fits the pattern of selective liberalism that has run through this book. The limits to current human rights policy reflect the more negative side of the internal-external spillover. Resources are increasingly squeezed, political power diminished, and the EU's own appeal as a rights-model under more critical scrutiny. Stepping down to concrete examples of policy implementation, the evidence presents a decidedly mixed record.

The Balkans

Even in the immediate neighborhood, trends have varied. Balkan activists insist this is one region in which the EU's gravity model retains pull and in which "approximation" with EU norms is still the metric driving reform. In June 2013, member states agreed to open accession talks with Serbia. Firm EU conditionality has helped get Albania's reform process back on track, with largely democratic elections held in June 2013. However, many aspects of European support have had a prejudicial impact The general feeling within EU discussions is that the crisis has made it likely that in practice Croatia will be the last new entrant for some time (even if Montenegro has already advanced notably in its accession negotiations). German politicians still insist that the EU should not "offend" Russia by moving too fast on Balkan accession. Popular distrust with the union is growing, according to official interlocutors from the region. They complain that delays to the process have already held back democratic deepening. The EU is berated for simply setting hurdles and offering little actively to help reformers overcome those conditions. Democracy funds to the Balkans have decreased during the recession.

Efforts at constitutional reform in Bosnia have given way to more stability-oriented policies. The United States complains that the EU has unhelpfully focused on what Bosnia needs to do to meet pre-entry legislative requirements rather than what it needs to do to make its political processes more sustainable.[61] Bosnia is increasingly fragile; democratic backsliding in each of its constituent parts has taken it further from functioning as a unitary state—the core precondition to advancing toward EU accession. The crisis has made Greece dig in its heels even more firmly against granting Macedonia accession talks as a reward for its democratic reform. The EU may have toughly warned that closing democratic space, the removal of opposition members from parliament in December 2012, and several months of tense government-opposition street protests put Macedonia's accession process at risk. But such pressure has been undermined by the fact that this process has anyway been stalled for six years—a delay many in the country see as contributing to growing instability. Similarly, with their own worsening secession-related problems domestically, the five EU member states that refuse to recognize Kosovo have delayed a pre-accession agreement with Pristina. The May 2013 EU-mediated Serb-Kosovar deal still faces many obstacles to resolve these problems. Any conversation with Balkan diplomats or civil society representatives soon turns to their complaints that the region is being overloaded with pre-accession harmonization requirements in excess of what previous applicants were asked to ingest and that provide multiple veto points for skeptics of enlargement to frustrate reform momentum.

Middle East

The Arab Spring has dragged some of the lethargy from the EU's Middle East policies. Several member states not only undertook military engagement in democracy's name in Libya but have retained a significant presence in that country's post-Qaddafi institution-building challenges. Tough sanctions have been imposed on Libya, Syria, and Yemen. More than a billion euros of new aid has been found to assist reform in North Africa and the Middle East, channeled mainly through the commission but also through member states' plethora of new democracy programs in the region. The EU has become more willing to withhold portions of this aid where human rights have worsened or long-promised democratic reforms have been delayed. European relations with Islamist parties have been largely normalized. European civil society initiatives today engage with a far wider range of interlocutors than previously. More generous trade access and mobility partnerships have been promised to Arab states as a reward for democratic advances.

Yet despite these policy changes, European governments have prevaricated on many aspects of democratic reform in North Africa and the Middle East. Aid amounts are still relatively limited. Many of the promised incentives, such as market access and labor mobility, are still being painstakingly negotiated three years into the Arab Spring. Many cases of tightened repression have not met with any European response. Security and stability continue to enjoy the same priority status in European policies toward the Gulf, Lebanon, and Algeria. European military cooperation with non-reforming Gulf monarchies has expanded dramatically since the Arab Spring erupted. Policy toward Iran has been largely limited to the nuclear dossier. Iraq's slide toward authoritarianism has not yet engendered any notable European engagement. In Jordan and Morocco, the EU continues to be content to shore up very limited processes of reform that do little to threaten the incumbent monarchs. Engagement with some parts of the Islamist spectrum remains limited, despite Salafi and other groups' bursting onto the mainstream political scene. Egypt provides the clearest example of European resources and incentives being insufficient to prompt recalcitrant elites to implement more far-reaching democratization; the EU criticized the army's retaking of power in July 2013 but did not change any of its policies as a consequence. While the UK and France have pushed to broaden support for the Syrian rebels, at the time of writing pressure has not been strong enough to dislodge the Bashar Assad regime.

Eastern States

In the Eastern dimension, support to democratic actors has registered some advances since the eurozone crisis started. In early 2013 Germany and Poland proposed to boost EU offers to Eastern partners, linked more tightly to democratic reforms, and even reopen the general prospects of accession across the region. Eastern states have benefited from the Arab Spring as new initiatives introduced after the uprisings have been applied to them as well. This is the case with the Neighborhood Civil Society Facility. The Eastern Partnership (EaP) now attracts more than 200 groups to its annual Civil Society Forum meetings. Over 2012 and 2013, national versions of the Civil Society Forum were set up in all six EaP members; a Comprehensive Institution Building program commenced; additional aid of 130 million euros was released to reward reforms in Moldova, Georgia, and Armenia; talks on visa facilitation and mobility partnerships advanced as a further positive incentive; and human rights dialogues were upgraded in each EaP state.[62]

In practice, the EU has struggled to find an effective balance of pressure and incentive with Ukraine. The EU has toughened pressure on Ukraine to revive democratic standards, suspending talks on a new trade agreement at the end of 2011 in response to the imprisonment of opposition leader Yulia Tymoshenko. The EU then criticized irregularities in Ukraine's parliamentary elections in October 2012, interference in the judiciary by Viktor Yanukovych's government, and the ruling family's extended control over many key state and economic positions.

European states have, however, done much to undercut their own leverage. Germany and a handful of other member states would not even allow Ukraine to define itself as "European" in its new agreement with the union, for fear that this would recognize its right to candidacy. The EU's message to Ukraine has increasingly been to forget membership and concentrate on "getting its own house in order." Ukrainian companies see the Deep and Comprehensive Free Trade Area Agreeements (DCFTA) as being too onerous in its requirements for regulatory harmonization—unlike Russia's Eurasian customs union offer.[63] Polish officials suspect that Germany has blocked association agreement talks for the ulterior motive of not wanting a debate about Ukrainian accession rather than as one component in a coherent democracy support strategy.

Conversely, Poland has wanted the bar lowered to dissuade Yanukovych from joining the customs union with Russia. Indeed, Poland has become the most pro-engagement member state in Ukraine. EU policy toward Ukraine is an uneasy balance between two contrasting aims—putting off membership candidacy and preventing the country from slipping into a Russian orbit—neither of which has any great interest in improving democratic standards per se. The tensions in EU policy contributed to Ukraine postponing preparations for the association agreement at the end of November 2013. Despite a sustained period of EU pressure, Yanukovych has continued to centralize power in an increasingly personalistic, superpresidential regime. As of this writing, the EU was deliberating how to respond to Ukraine's decision and the civic protests it unleashed.

A new initiative specifically targets support to Belarusian activists. The EU has significantly increased civil society support to Belarus since 2010. In Georgian parliamentary elections in October 2012, the United National Movement, the ruling party of the increasingly autocratic president Mikheil Saakashvili, was defeated, with several European embassies playing a clear role in ensuring that power was transferred democratically. In another positive case, reforming Moldova has benefited from a raft of EU programs as it has overtaken Ukraine in the pecking order of relations with the union: it now stands ready for a reform-deepening EaP association agreement.

But even in these cases, many have criticized EU policies. After Georgia's 2012 elections, some observers accused the EU of double standards, as it sharply criticized democratic imperfections it had overlooked under the pro-Saakashvili administration. It is still not clear whether the EU approaches Georgia through a lens of norms or competing spheres of influence with Russia. In a not dissimilar vein, one Moldovan ambassador laments that the state of democracy has been rendered more precarious by member states holding back a firm accession promise, in part due to a reluctance to press Russia to cede its line on Transnistria. And local reformers trying to work in Belarus still upbraid the EU for being unwilling to impose a full range of sanctions against the Lukashenko regime or offer meaningful, direct support to democrats. In Belarus the disparate strands of engagement and ostracism almost risk neutralizing each other.

Russia

Even key members of the German government have begun to speak out against the human rights abuses that have become more serious in Russia since Vladimir Putin's return to the presidency. Angela Merkel made a point of reversing recent German policy to meet with opposition figures on her November 2012 visit to Moscow. The EU has also launched a tough new antitrust case against Gazprom, forcing it to separate out the supply and transport arms of its operations in Europe. An EU-Russia Civil Society Forum has been established in Prague. And the EU-Russia summit in June 2013 was frosty; pressure from the European Parliament sufficed to hold up an offer of visa liberalization to Russia on human rights grounds.

However, European governments have judged it too risky to offer any significant backing to the new wave of democratic protests in Russia. When the U.S. Agency for International Development was ejected from Russia in September 2012, European aid agencies escaped attention because they were seen as much less intent on supporting critical civil society voices. When in late 2012 the United States adopted sanctions on Russian officials involved in the killing of an imprisoned activist, Sergei Magnitsky, European governments expressly declined to follow suit. Diplomats define the EU-Russia Modernization Partnership as dead, because Putin's idea of "modernization" is entirely statist-authoritarian. Indeed, this initiative is seen as having become "a vehicle for member states to further their business interests."[64] EU-Russia trade reached record levels in 2012. The EU opened talks on visa liberalization just as Putin clamped down on democrats. One northern European (and generally, liberal) minister captures the consensus mood in insisting that more business integration is the priority in relations with Russia.

The softening in Poland's approach toward Russia has been particularly striking. The Donald Tusk government has been partly concerned that the country's previous anti-Moscow fixation was proving counterproductive within the EU. It wishes to keep in step with Germany in the east. The general sentiment among diplomats is that a tough response to renewed repression is pointless as it will simply push Russia toward China's orbit. The mood music surrounding the December 2012 EU-Russia summit returned to a familiar asymmetry: while Herman Van Rompuy emphasized his hope that "together the EU and Russia can make a decisive contribution to global governance and regional conflict resolution," President Putin came directly from a summit where he urged former Soviet states to band together to neutralize Western influence. Even when Russian authorities raided the offices of German party foundations, the EU response was muted. By spring 2013, conditionality was reversed, as the EU courted Russia for funds to bail out Cyprus. The most respected Russia experts argue that all this reflects the reality that Putin's Russia has now slipped firmly outside the orbit of significant European influence.[65]

Asia

Burma/Myanmar is a case where the EU has invested much to demonstrate its continued commitment to liberal political values. In response to Burma's political opening, member states struck a balance between positive responses and continued pressure on the regime. Sanctions were partially lifted early on and then suspended for one year in April 2012, with their permanent lifting made conditional on the release of political prisoners. GSP trade preferences were not reinstated, as reports on International Labor Organization standards remained negative. The EU has provided funds to support a human rights commission, with the aim to give this body more independence. EU Development Commissioner Andris Piebalgs paid an early visit and promised support for administrative, judicial, and police reforms, on top of basic development assistance. Through their renewed engagement, several member states have supported reform of the informal economy in Burma's border areas, recognizing that sustainable reform requires more than simply supporting Aung San Suu Kyi against the generals. The EU has focused on citizenship rights, funding a new peace and mediation center to the tune of 700,000 euros for mediation among ethnic groups. The EU is also offering support for ASEAN to play a primary role in standard setting for human rights that would reduce the risk of Burma's reforms being reversed. Member states agreed to lift sanctions in April 2013 and offered a range of new cooperation, including debt relief and GSP benefits: this was generally felt to be a correct response, even though human rights NGOs have criticized Western governments for moving too fast in search of lucrative resource contracts.[66]

Across Asia more generally, however, democracy promotion is still highly circumscribed. One of the least surprising effects of the crisis is that few remnants remain of anything amounting to a serious European human rights policy toward China. The diminution of EU efforts to raise human rights concerns with China has been widely observed and chronicled. While Angela Merkel has on occasion spoken out on human rights more vociferously than her predecessors, her visit in February 2012 was especially criticized for soft-pedaling on political reform issues, with the chancellor accepting a ban on meeting human rights activists. China has sought to dilute the frequency of the human rights dialogue and steer its focus away from individual cases of human rights abuses. In fact, the Chinese government no longer allows the human rights dialogue to take place in China. Only a handful of European leaders continue to meet the Dalai Lama; when they are castigated by China in reprimand, they gain no solidarity from their EU partners. China suspended high-level meetings with the UK after David Cameron met with the Dalai Lama in May 2012; what the British government presents as a stand of principle is seen by other member states as London's self-marginalization in Beijing, and an invitation for China to play divide and rule.

An EU-China people-to-people initiative commenced in April 2012 and has led to concrete exchanges, but it also has been complicated by some member states' visa requirements on Chinese visits. The main EU aim has been to push for a new rule of law dialogue; the Chinese government has been more amenable to this focus, as the established human rights dialogue has hit a brick wall of ineffectiveness. Germany has its own well-developed rule of law dialogue running since 2002, which has shared experience mainly on legal rules for a market economy. The UK also works on judicial reform. Member states coordinate on being present at human rights trials and provide some technical and capacity building, for example on rule of law issues with the Chinese police academy. Projects to support civil society have, diplomats reveal, taken a more practical hue, focusing on service provision as opposed to such overtly politically driven organizations. The EU's village governance project was stopped in 2006, and no efforts have been made to resume its widely lauded work. Critics say that democracy has become a "non-issue" in the EU's relations with China.[67]

More broadly in the region, it appears that the EU has gradually accepted the much-lauded "Asian way." The EU has opened trade talks with Vietnam without requiring democratic reforms. While Herman Van Rompuy spoke out plainly on his 2012 trip to Vietnam against the detention of artists, Vietnam nevertheless has benefited from sizable gains in EU aid, and the EU will continue to be the country's biggest donor up to 2020 even as it reaches middle-income status without political liberalization. In Cambodia, the commission's trade directorate blocked a member state proposal to remove trade preferences on human rights grounds. The values debate is addressed in a nonconfrontational way through human rights dialogues. But all sides agree these are rather formalistic and devoid of tangible results. Democracy assistance in Asia is more curtailed than in other regions. The EU-ASEAN partnership on democracy and fundamental rights remains thin on substance. On human rights, no more than a few exchanges have been supported to help the ASEAN Intergovernmental Commission on

Human Rights. No new funds have been forthcoming for human rights. NGOs criticized the EU for welcoming unconditionally the 2012 ASEAN human rights declaration.

CONCLUSION

In line with analytical doubts over the fate of the liberal order, Europe's response to the crisis has not been in a singular direction. Indeed, this internal-external link has become increasingly difficult to manage in recent years. Ad hoc selectivity has become prominent. The eurozone crisis has on occasion increased the EU's resolve to defend the liberal order, but has also often encouraged a retreat from such firm normative commitment.

Some efforts have been forthcoming to maintain the momentum behind support for multilateralism, liberal security, democracy, and human rights, and even to ratchet up existing policy tools. In some areas, however, a general weakening of the EU's cosmopolitan spirit is evident. Policymakers of course still lay claim to its core values. But many assume the future will be one of little more than a residual or even pseudo-liberalism, hanging on stubbornly through merely formal commitments as the world heads in a fundamentally different direction. While European commitments to supporting democracy have advanced in admirable ways, policymakers express as much doubt as enthusiasm over the impact of international democratization. A line is still heard frequently that democracy often cannot be supported because it risks intensifying threats and instability. While such caution has much merit, it fails to recognize that democratization tends to have insidious effects when it is unsuccessful more than when it is successful—dangers are attributed to an excess of democracy support that in fact may flow more from its dearth.

A move is under way from high-principled multilateralism to more pragmatic alliances. Multilateralism no longer seems targeted quite so directly at a set of unadulterated or unmediated global commons. While "minilateralism" is in some ways a sensible and practical way forward, it has often been unclear whether it is pursued as a tactic to build support for liberal norms in a more incremental fashion or as a means of more substantively circumventing the principles of liberal order. Recent changes in EU policy suggest that the jury is still out on this question. There is certainly a risk that understandings of European identities are contracting and being defined in more exclusivist terms against the outside world. Faced with severe challenges from what some label the "Bismarckian" rising powers, the temptation is clearly for the EU to follow suit. At a minimum it is clear that European governments are hedging. Tested by an eclectic mix of paradigms, they seek to keep rules-based cooperation going, but in more flexible and ad hoc ways. This has kept a degree of liberal solidarity in play and much multilateral cooperation alive. But does such an ambivalent mishmash of strategic logics represent a sustainable long-term strategy? It is to this question of the best way forward that the concluding chapter now turns.

CHAPTER 7

CONCLUSION: REDESIGNING GLOBAL EUROPE

Europe's crisis has not been and does not need to be apocalyptically negative for European foreign policies. It would be exaggerated to paint the EU as a stricken Paradise Lost, set for dusty, anachronistic oblivion. Positive, global ambition is still appropriate. Robert Kagan reminds us that the United States has always been caught in a struggle to stay influential and appeal as a model; there was never a halcyon zenith of perfectly effective power from which the United States now declines.[1] In some sense, this could be said to be even truer of Europe, in terms of both the time-stretched vicissitudes of the integration process and national foreign policies that have already passed through the post-colonial humbling of power retraction. In mitigation, European governments have begun to inch toward a more coherent and proactive geopolitical vision to navigate the choppier waters of a crisis-reshuffled world order. After summarizing the book's findings on how EU external relations have responded to the crisis, this concluding chapter outlines some of the challenges that such a vision is likely to encounter. As Europe recovers from its fiscal rehab, how should it position itself in the world?

THE LEGACY OF CRISIS

The crisis has bequeathed an EU that is more vulnerable and less self-assured. The Damoclean sword of relative decline hangs a little more menacingly over Europe's baleful glance. In the darkest days of the crisis, the EU stared for the first time at the merest possibility of its own mortality—an experience that was, as any such realization, shuddering in its disorientation and concentrating of mind. The crisis has tainted the spirit as well as the material. The EU now often appears to be buffeted by the tide of global affairs more than charting its own course through these challenges. It is more importuning than compass setting. The EU no longer bestrides the world, or even its own neighborhood. Conscious of its need for international support, the EU is a less contrarian power. The crisis has bred a less imperious and less intemperate Europe.

A wider temporal perspective adds little comfort. 2014's centenary of the First World War provides a sobering reference point. A century of self-inflicted destruction dislodged European nations from the pinnacle of their global power; in fighting each other, European powers all lost out to a resurgent East. And now, in the distended shadow of this long sweep of decline, in what seem less dramatic and disruptive times, deep economic crisis once more evokes the ghosts of discord. The past decade has been especially humbling for the UK as the country suffered military embarrassments in Iraq and Afghanistan, sinking its reputation in the one area of policy where it continued to punch above its weight; saw its overdependence on financial services brutally punished in the economic crisis; and now stumbles myopically toward marginalization within Europe.

Of course, the EU can recover its economic footing; rising powers may well falter; and effective European influence can recuperate even as other powers gain long-term structural weight in the international system. Yet, even if all this occurs, the pain and costs have been too great to reduce Europe's predicament to no more than a temporary and even fortuitously redeeming parenthesis.

While the lesions run deep, not all is grim and faithless retreat. There is a spillover from the internal crisis, but the effectiveness of European foreign policy should not be seen as entirely dependent on any particular redesign of EU institutions. Even a rolling back of some internal post-

Maastricht commitments need not take Europe back to disastrously conflictive relations. The EU is neither declining nor improving wholesale; dynamics differ depending on the policy area. Headline conclusions from the preceding chapters highlight this balance:

- Economic crisis has for now (late 2013) been calmed, but without qualitative improvement to the model of integration or a solution to the EU's seriously aggravated "democracy problem."

- The crisis has left a serious dent in EU global influence but has also spurred efforts at compensatory coordination and revived ambition.

- The crisis has pushed the EU to be a more geoeconomic actor, in some welcome, and some less beneficial, ways.

- The EU has invested huge effort during the crisis to correct its erstwhile neglect of Asia's rise and has tentatively felt its way toward a more balanced economic and political relationship with this ascendant region.

- The EU has belatedly realized that greater effort is required to keep a liberal world order intact, yet it flits between commitment to and doubt over the viability of this order.

The book's core message is that the spillover from internal crisis to the external sphere is significant, but it is also more variegated than might have been assumed. The book has charted how this is the case in relation to foreign economic policy, the question of who controls EU foreign policy, and the place of liberal democratic values in external strategies—these three areas being related to the three components of the internal crisis dissected in chapter two. The chapters have shown how the nature of internal economic crisis management has pushed EU external policies in a number of new directions, especially in the sphere of geoeconomics. They have also demonstrated how the EU's own democracy challenge has reverberated on its traditional foreign policy approaches to liberal rights. And they have highlighted how Germany's changing role has become a new focus of debate, whether in relation to incipient German leadership, a mismatch between the country's internal dominance and external caution, or German bilateral alliances with other medium-sized global powers.

Some improvements to external policy unity are emerging even in the dark-day guardedness of financial turmoil. The crisis has deepened both unity and bilateralism; the EU's foreign policy, while fractured, has not degenerated entirely. Even as recrimination and division have racked the endless procession of crisis summits, the patterns of regular coordination in many areas of external relations have quietly advanced. The crisis has not completely inverted established EU foreign policy identities. The EU still labors to avert the excesses of Darwinian multipolarity. After so much suffering, the official "crisis-as-opportunity" panegyric is impolitic; yet the EU has done much to appease its often-insincere critics. Postcrisis European foreign policies are not entirely bereft of liberal cosmopolitan values. Rather the chapters suggest the emergence of a more selective and rationalized form of liberalism.

Tying together the trends across different policy areas—economic and political; in rising powers and failing states; in the near and far abroad— the new guiding tenet of European foreign policies seems to be this: more selective international effort and incursion into global leadership, with European governments keener than before to justify such involvement in terms of tangible gain. The EU has not entirely lost its normative bearings, but the tone of its approach to the question of international values has shifted. Although some values-based strategies have held their ground, the aftermath of the crisis must put to rest claims that the EU is a congenitally ethical-liberal power, resistant to nefarious and feckless pursuit of its interests. The crisis has not completely quelled the EU's self-referential self-esteem; a residue lives on, especially in those immediately peripheral states where many still see a natural Euro-sphere. But diplomats have begun to appreciate the issue of values in a slightly more varied and decentered fashion. Where backing for liberal political values has strengthened, it has been in response to domestically driven demands and reforms in countries beyond Europe's borders. And, at the same time, the values of multilateral problem solving, interdependence, and collective security are pursued in a way that is more attuned to concrete, beneficial policy outcomes.

While the crisis has driven areas of more intense foreign policy activity, the preceding chapters reveal a more selective set of international commitments. Despite the fragile green shoots of cooperative political will, many in the EU still appear tempted by the siren of disengaged introspection.

European Union officials themselves lament how strategic thinking has still been muddied by familiar "competence struggles." A residue of parochialism that the Lisbon Treaty was supposed to banish persists. Herman Van Rompuy's speechwriter again puts its well: prominent EU leaders have yet to learn how to "speak for Europe, not EU institutions." A fixation with internal institutional design endures. The final report of the Future of Europe Group of the eleven foreign ministers made no mention at all of the substance of foreign policy, only institutional reform options several decades old—as if the strategic dimensions of the crisis could somehow be reduced to the need for more majority voting, slightly more power for the high representative over commissioners, or a new ranking of senior and junior commissioners.[2]

Governments' realist calculations have both spurred and sapped European unity. Weakness has encouraged member states to reinforce some areas of cooperation. But the divergences engendered by internal crisis have also driven member states to break ranks and secure quick-gain benefits for their own national interest. In aspects of their commercial and geostrategic policies, member states have broken from their European partners and given greater preference to maximizing bilateral interest; national self-help has been a powerful recurring theme of governments' crisis response. Simultaneously, however, member states have invested in strengthening the common European dimensions of the way that relations with pivotal rising powers are managed. Member states have artfully sought to combine the advantages of convergence and divergence. While it was ever thus, the impact of the crisis is significant in having intensified efforts on both sides of the equation. This means that reconciling the often barely reconcilable requires greater exertion. The more ruthless and unsentimental pursuit of interest has produced some very contradictory policy recipes.

A feeling has taken root that in some regions and in some policy areas, "masterly inactivity" may in its prudence be a wiser play than a blanket liberal ardor. It is in this way that the squeeze between internal crisis and global-systemic reordering expresses itself. With such widespread antipathy to the West, the EU may judge that it is paradoxically more likely to get what it wants the less it is seen to be trying to do so. In conversation with European diplomats, a frustrated sentiment often boils over, challenging the ebullient and self-confident rising powers "to show that they can do better in running the global order." It is ironic that the EU now lacks the power to get its way, even as non-Western powers complain that the international system is still too Eurocentric. The EU is berated for a normative dominance that in fact it no longer possesses in equal measure. All this nourishes arguments for the union to focus on defending its own immediate interests rather than investing vainly in a besieged liberal world framework.[3]

The postcrisis trend is toward a more unsentimental multilateralism and a more selective and rationalized form of cosmopolitan liberalism. Mapping out the shifts in postcrisis geopolitics is rendered both more hazardous and more imperative. Joseph Nye argues that such challenges can be met only by "smart power," based on a form of "liberal realism" that links together harder and softer elements of power.[4] Europe's response so far has been not so much of smart power as of makeshift power. While the wounded EU shows some laudable resolve to be an influential medium power, many aspects of its response to this crisis have amplified concerns over the coherence of its global policy.

With less leverage, European liberal foreign policies have become more selective, seeking to distinguish between those norms that "really matter" and those seen as an "ethical luxury." Much of the EU's new humility may be humbug. But there has been a modicum of genuine willingness to listen to others and not quite so automatically to assume that spreading rights and prosperity is in the gift of an EU asked simply to reproduce itself around the globe. Governments and diplomats exhibit some recognition that the EU is today less able to exert influence, as other states are no longer content to be supine supplicants of its aid and trade access.

Others' perceptions of the EU and its global presence have dived as precipitously as European economic indicators. While European policymakers insist, with some justification, that the EU has come to adopt a more humble tone, this change does not yet seem to have been fully picked up outside the continent. Many around the world today speak of the crisis-stricken EU as if it were a reliquary of idealism more than shining Kantian city on the hill. Europe today appears as derided as it was by many deified.

If others see Europe to be weaker than it really is, this matters as it renders influence harder. Many European policymakers and analysts insist that the EU has gained new plaudits for its innovation in managing what is essentially a global rather than euro-specific crisis of rebalancing; they argue that the EU has in fact cultivated a more positive image by virtue of finding institutionally cooperative means of mitigating the crisis ahead of others. Whether this is entirely convincing to the rest of world is debatable. The EU long asked the world to admire it for the unsinkable ship it navigated; it now claims to be a model for the way it deals with that same ship taking on water. As the EU's standard self-image is increasingly divorced from its reality, others' credulity has worn thinner.

A "MULTIPOLAR LIBERALISM"

So, what is the way forward? There is much genuine concern that the crisis represents an inflection point in the liberal world order. The prospect is undoubtedly real. This has bred a normative uncertainty that gives the impression of the EU being a contrite, even dissolute power. For the solemn realist, postcrisis Europe stands closer to an inevitable return to history's unremitting brutality: European peace and cooperation in the late twentieth century was a small patch of blue in a tempest-filled sky—that is now closing over. It has become increasingly fashionable for analysts to suggest that an apparently overly ethical EU must "move away from Kant and toward Machiavelli." In particular, the belief persists that the lesson of southern Europe's ruination is that further enlargement should not now be considered as a tool to help non-EU states consolidate democratic norms.[5] Long-time critics of European liberalism argue that the crisis renders the EU's pretensions to be a global player even more untenable, while also straining even further its own multiculturalism.[6] Europe's crisis cannot be separated from the health of the liberal world order; the crisis itself renders the liberal world order more difficult to maintain.[7]

However, true prudence requires the EU to retain some degree of internationalist agenda. The more Europe seeks to mimic the geopolitical behavior of established or emerging powers, the more it undermines its comparative advantage. While assertive geoeconomics is entirely proper, casting commercial policies in narrowly mercantilistic terms may not serve the EU's own long-term interests. The current approach to exiting recession and recouping a presence in rising powers may prove too utilitarian to constitute good geostrategy. It is vital to strike alliances with rising powers, but the EU has begun to strike its bargains on extremely expedient terms. There is a meaningful difference between seeking reciprocity of rules and reciprocity of merely material benefits. The UN warns that multilateral bodies need to develop guidelines to manage the bewildering array of commercial and strategic subregional accords toward a "coherent pluralism."[8] Measured against this canon, the EU's liberal ambivalence shows fickle fealty to an admirable vision.

The EU was slow in reacting to the shift in power away from the West. Arguably, it now rather overstates the weight of polarity in its external strategies. Many insiders fear that a Europe dominated by economically focused Germany could become unduly mercantile and less politically engaged globally. International policy must be understood in its most expansive ramifications. As the crisis shunts the EU even more decisively beyond the historical apex of its power, the union needs multilaterally enshrined rules more, not less. Such ideals must not be left orphaned by the crisis. One of the strong points of EU foreign policy was its early recognition that geoeconomics and geopolitics cannot be separated; to countenance such a separation now would represent an unfortunate regression. In the tumultuous blizzard of the crisis, the EU has sometimes given the impression of forgetting what it already knew.

The challenge is not to abandon the union's commitment to liberal values but to update it. While it may be argued that cosmopolitan values are in the EU's own long-term interest, the union will need to approach and support such values in a different and less judgmental fashion. A cosmopolitan European foreign policy should be built on sobriety rather than missionary zeal. Certainly, erstwhile notions of "liberal imperialism" must be ditched. A liberalism compatible with and attuned to a more multipolar world is required. A middle-line liberalism needs normative actions to be rationalized by and grounded in calculations of tangible interests. Ulrich Beck's cosmopolitan realism is a useful anchor: it advocates the pursuit of self-interest rather than a mushy moralism, but it also calls for those interests to be understood with a broader community in mind.[9]

The crisis has nudged the EU toward developing what might be termed a multipolar liberalism. European governments have tried to walk the thin line between over- and underreaction. They have sought a balanced mix of cooperative realism and cosmopolitan internationalism. The future challenge will be to put flesh on the bones of this nascent policy framework. Many EU documents offer tentative, generic guidelines for an active medium power that is internationalist in its engagement, cosmopolitan in its values, able to cast utilitarian bilateralism within a framework of mutually beneficial multilateral cooperation, and up to the task of balancing the big rising powers with challenges in its own neighborhood. Understanding what these guidelines mean in practice and effectively implementing a multipolar liberalism will entail four challenges:

1. Democratic cooperation. First, a clear legacy of the eurozone crisis is that effective support for the liberal world order will depend even more on partnering with rising democracies such as Brazil, India, South Africa, Indonesia, South Korea, and Turkey. This should not entail exclusivist clubs of democracies, but practical, low-key cooperation on liberal values. A deal is required: the West needs to accept that it cannot separate efforts to promote liberal values from the broader injustices of the prevailing international configuration of power, but rising democracies should not let complaints about unjust historical legacies impede the North-South cooperation needed by people in danger around the world. European states must accept a loss of power in multilateral bodies as the price for restoring credibility to the liberal world order.

European governments have begun to move in this direction. The new theme among some European donors is that of North-South-South or triangular cooperation, the EU teaming up with a rising democracy to work together in a poorer third country. For example, the UK has used some of its aid resources to work with Brazil in poorer African states. The British development agency and the French Foreign Ministry both have units for partnerships with rising powers on reform initiatives. The Open Government Partnership, kicked off under a U.S.-Brazil partnership, handed over to an Indonesia-UK lead in 2012, and is pursuing peer review of each participating state's transparency initiatives.

Rising democracies remain cautious in their cooperation with Western powers. But their views are evolving. Differences have emerged between Turkey and Indonesia, on the one hand, and Brazil, India, and South Africa, on the other. The latter three still tend to be more reluctant to draw a line under European colonial abuses and begin cooperation "from a clean slate." Interestingly, these governments are now under more criticism from their own NGOs for their realist stances abroad. Brazil adopts very different tactics but shares basic liberal values.[10] Even India has begun to adopt a slightly more active external posture, working, for example, through its own International Institute of Democracy and Election Management.

As a result of the crisis, the BRICs have come more aggressively to belittle the EU, with a heavy dose of schadenfreude. The EU retorts equally tartly that these states may criticize Western efforts but still bring little to the table of global problem solving. Diplomats in Brussels mutter angrily about the euro crisis being used to mask others' shortcomings. Much is image: the rising powers justifiably want to feel that they are shaping norms. One Indonesian diplomat maps a route forward: the EU needs to learn to "sit in the back" when partnering with other powers on liberal value initiatives rather than publicizing how these reflect a new European tutelage over North-South partnerships. Brazil's "Responsibility while protecting" may be slightly different from the "Responsibility to protect" concept, but shows an interest in contributing new ideas. Some insist that in states like Brazil there are the first signs of a pullback in anti-Western nationalism as policymakers wonder who will be providing global public goods in the future. Sensitive but determined diplomacy and recast democracy initiatives might be able to tease out such positive potential. The challenge for the EU will be how to offer itself as a comprehensive partner in a way that China and other states cannot and how to make sure this is an asset of greater comparative advantage in the future.

2. Shaping power. Second, the focus is likely to be on how to shape agendas. In the future the EU and its member states may be less able to guarantee particular and specific liberal outcomes, but they can still aspire to shape the basic tenets that guide international problem solving. Instead of sticking with the usual rising-versus-declining powers or West-versus-the-Rest dichotomies, the challenge will be to increase the number of powers that are engaged rather than introverted. If the EU can help shape the tenets of future order in this broad direction, partnerships for global problem solving are more likely to fall into place. In 2012 the German Foreign Ministry produced a paper defining a "shaping power."[11] One senior German planner insists this shaping role is potent below the level of states and that creeping individual empowerment positions the EU well by playing to its sociological strengths. A barometer of EU "shaping power" could be compiled to help move mental maps beyond the self-referential and institutionally heavy ways in which the union has traditionally defined its influence. Despite the crisis, Europe remains less fractious internally than many other regions and thus still has the policy space to "shape outward."

The German effort on shaping power is extremely promising; work remains to be done to determine what this means in operational terms and whether as currently conceived it is indeed liberal norms that are to be "shaped." Encouragingly, Germany and the UK appear to share a largely outward-looking global vision, more than some other member states and despite everything else that currently divides Berlin and London. To create effective "shaping platforms," it has been argued that Europe's model of multilateral cooperation needs to build in more flexible networks of civic and business experts and stakeholders in a flatter organizational structure better adapted to today's fast-moving challenges.[12] Jolyon Howorth stresses that the EU still needs to move away from traditional, Westphalian alliances, since influence derives more from multifaceted cooperation and connectedness.[13] The European Commission suggests that an ethos of "trans-institutionalism" is imperative.[14] Influence should be seen less in terms of sanctions and punitive conditionality; the evidence from many quantitative studies reports that while these practices have helped in containing regimes, they are far less effective at fostering domestic political change.[15] Partnerships are essential, but different types of partnerships must be distinguished from each other: alliances struck because of shared fears must give way to broader commitments to work together to shape agendas. The EU needs to debate how to attain such shaping power at a forum away from summits and councils that oblige ministers to focus on immediate crises rather than this long-term imperative.

This is the ground on which future European partnership with China should be measured out. Chinese academics talk about the notion of China as a bridge-building, mediating power; this may offer at least a modicum of commonality with a prospective European shaping power. Chinese intellectuals define the balance in Beijing's outlook thus: China wants only very incremental changes to the current order and prefers "reform from within" rather than rupture to a whole new system, but it will hedge if the West does not move with the times. While confrontational strands of opinion exist within the Communist Party, for the moment China is not opposed to the liberal world order per se, so much as the Western tendency to blame Beijing for all illiberal ills, when its own record of defending human rights and multilateral fairness is so lacking. Without minimizing the magnitude of the challenge, this may indicate that at least a sliver of common ground is available on which Europe can entice China into a benign shaping of future norms. State-capitalist powers will not cede realpolitik until they feel multilateral institutions are more justly responsive to their positions.

3. *Beyond Europeanization.* Third, in the aftermath of the crisis it is surely even more necessary for the EU to move beyond the tendency to equate liberalism with Europeanization. Much of European liberal power has derived from the EU's extending its own forms of shared-regulatory governance beyond the union's formal frontiers. The EU's support for the liberal world order has been synonymous with a form of post-modern governance. This kind of geopolitics of regulatory osmosis, of Europeanization-as-benign-envelopment, has come to be deployed as almost co-extensive with normative power. While this will remain a pivotal dimension of European power, after the crisis it needs also to be recast. In a new book, Anthony Giddens argues that the EU must "drop its flight from power," having mistakenly thought for so long that the appeal of its own model exonerates the union from needing to exert more active forms of influence.[16] The combination of internal and external constraints outlined in this book suggests that the EU will need to think less in terms of European governance and more in terms of cosmopolitan governance. The EU must move from "replicating itself" to using its own achievements to influence jointly forged universalism. This is a subtle but important change not just for the EU but also for the rest of the world.

The EU's rules retain appeal. But the EU's push to externalize its own norms and standards is also more assertively resisted today, as it is perceived to be a strategy for corralling other states speciously into a sphere of administrative tutelage. Multilateralism needs to arise from local forums of interdependence, to which the EU, as one actor among many, then lends its support. The EU awaits its Copernican revolution, to break the mental map of layers of surrounding neighborhoods revolving around the unmoving pivot of the union.

The EU has taken some steps toward a less Euro-institutionalist approach. However, pinned against the ropes of financial crisis in some areas, the EU has actually clung more firmly to its own familiar institutional templates, while retreating from apparently expendable universalist agendas. The European Commission proudly boasts that more than 100 subcommittees function under the standard agreements it operates in the EU's neighborhood policy, reflecting what it insists is "the worldwide acceptance of the EU regulatory model."[17] Formal reports still tend to advocate more export of EU regulations as the main platform for strategic projection—without any mention of anything having gone at all wrong with the EU's model or with European foreign and security policy.[18] The EU remains guilty of much institutional mimetism: it assumes that reforms genuinely needed for a democratic process are the same as those needed simply to approximate very particular EU laws.[19] A truly liberal policy must not sell democracy as a definitive end-state aligned with "Western templates" but as a means of opening up local choices to influence political identities.

    4. Post-hegemonic transatlanticism. Fourth, the EU will need to consider how to recast a liberal transatlanticism for the post-Western world. The financial crisis has made it clear that the United States may not indefinitely be able to bear the cost of maintaining a liberal world order, through security guarantees and other international public goods.[20] To preserve the transatlantic relationship as the bedrock of the liberal world order, the EU must help the United States in the direction of a less hegemonic liberal internationalism. Worryingly, policy has drifted away from this pivotal strategic imperative. Notwithstanding the TTIP and some new EU-U.S. cooperation on China-related issues, consultation is thin on the need for a shared systemic vision of the reshaped global order. During the crisis, the liberal narrative has almost disappeared from the transatlantic partnership. The EU and the United States are more deeply entwined economically, but their strategic partnership wanes.[21] Both the EU and the United States now talk of a more selective transatlantic partnership, one that is more pragmatic and whose policy issues are more varied. Each berates the other for lack of leadership. When Hillary Clinton gave a keynote speech on priorities for the transatlantic relationship at the beginning of President Obama's second term, the focus was again on a list of concrete areas of cooperation, devoid of overarching principles for a remolded world order.[22] Officials on both sides of the Atlantic now advocate a narrow agenda, focused on selective economic cooperation to assist postcrisis recovery. For all the talk of global EU-U.S. global partnership, in 2013 the focus was back on long-debated transatlantic trade talks. As one senior diplomat puts it: the EU and the United States think similarly on many issues but are still uncertain over "the big direction."

The two partners compete with each other to curry favor with rising powers, almost willfully compounding each other's decline. Talking to U.S. officials, it is striking how they see the EU as useful in terms of bringing resources to the table for discrete issues, not as a partner for redesigning the global order. One (now former) official acknowledges that a "transatlantic conversation has not even started" on the rules that should govern the reshaped international system. Both the EU and the United States now tend to see the partnership in terms of the other helping cover for its own lowered ambitions. President Obama's reelection was met with justifiable relief across Europe but has not reversed these trends.

The way that U.S. liberal internationalism plays out will be a determining factor for the global order. The European vision of the liberal world order has tended to be different from the U.S. understanding that it is indistinguishable from an American-led order. There is still a tendency for both left and right in the United States to see the liberal world order as a function of American power. Conservative realists insist that peace, international cooperation, open trade, and democracy all rely on U.S. power.[23] The U.S. version of liberal internationalism is increasingly Jacksonian, predicated on selective international engagement, molded to concrete interests.[24] Thomas Carothers reveals how the Obama administration has eschewed framing democracy promotion as "universal grand strategy."[25] Forceful pleas have been made for the United States to adopt a less "exceptionalist" and hegemonic stance and help form a less hierarchical and more socially liberal community of "democratic internationalism."[26] But even these most progressive of U.S. visions still insist that the liberal order is inseparable from American leadership and that U.S. elites must be convinced that the constraints of internationalism can actually serve specific, interest-rooted end goals. They still inflate American leadership as the indispensable keystone of the liberal order.[27] The emerging risk is that its own domestic politics and insecurities are keeping the United States even more wedded to a traditional concept of its own power projection.

The EU's postcrisis challenge will be to convince the United States that a liberal world order based on a broader range of actors having a controlling stake is likely to be more firmly rooted than one associated with American interests. One could rebut the conservative realist argument by asking whether cavalier and injudiciously instrumental U.S. power in fact explains the very fragility of the liberal order that those same writers allude to, and whether more jointly shaped rules would not help extend its roots more deeply. The EU still needs to pull the United States into a more rules-based approach, consonant with the reshaped world order. And in order to have that influence, it will need to convince the United States that it is a serious security partner. The U.S. vision of a G2 in which it does battle for the "liberal side" is not a comfortable or auspicious one for the EU. The EU's challenge will be to help the United States retain influence not through hard power but through its management of the very networks and multiplicity of connections to which emerging powers so keenly desire access.[28] A familiar claim is that the EU promotes liberal values in the sense of inclusive international processes of dialogue and consultation, in marked contrast to the U.S. focus on liberal "end points."[29] If the EU is to live up to this noble self-image, it needs to put some backbone behind a transatlantic shaping of post-hegemonic liberal internationalism.

HUMBLED ADJUSTMENT

The crisis-afflicted world is replete with both risk and opportunity. The crisis brings about tectonic shifts in trade and resource distribution but not (yet) in war and peace as crises did in previous centuries. The new, post-Western order is not a completed canvas. The way that the EU acts now will condition how other states respond. With so much of the emerging order in indeterminate flux, it must for now be overly defeatist to reduce the effort invested in supporting cosmopolitan universalism. The West failed to see the rise of the BRICs; it should not now become so fixated on the rise of China and other powers that it misses the trend toward diverse polycentrism. Too much idealism may look out of touch; but too much value-neutral realpolitik is overly reductive in its understanding of global trends.

The context beyond the euro crisis retains some qualities of buoyancy. The EU may be less able to shape specific outcomes, but its relative decline occurs within an order based largely on peaceful interdependence, which is what the union has always sought—precisely as its insurance against crisis. A world of more equal power may be no bad thing for Europe. The EU can craft many positive outcomes in a world that houses a higher number of prosperous markets and internationally engaged powers that are potential partners. But foreign policy after the crisis must cope with increased uncertainty and instability. As the many types of insecurity interact more tightly, the amplifying effects of economic and political turmoil expand. Greater precision, foresight, and understanding of the good and bad of the crisis aftershock are still called for.

A more decentered liberalism would run with the grain of a multi-nodal, polycentric world order. It would be based on a defense of the irreducible core of liberal values while leaving scope for institutional variations across other regions and cultures. Tzvetan Todorov argues that the true spirit of the enlightenment that is in need of rescue is that of freeing up society to find its own consensus and not to prescribe the content of either religious or secular-ideological beliefs.[30] This all points toward a kind of "reform liberalism," which charts a course between laissez-faire and dirigiste-collectivist policies and suggests that solutions lie not in less liberalism but in a more complete conjoining of economic freedoms with effectively empowering social and political freedoms.[31] A liberalism, in other words, that is more accepting of variation, more about setting broad parameters for economic and political comportment, not quite so pugnaciously Promethean.

The reshaped world order is an uncertain place but has not yet produced major, tangible, or direct military threats, meaning that cash-strapped governments are struggling to make the case for hefty defense budgets to their populations and parliaments. The argument increasingly has to be made to persuade many EU policymakers to remain strongly committed to outward-looking, internationalist strategic engagement. A crucial point to make is that this is not just a question of changes in the EU per se but in national foreign policy outlooks, too. Weaker national foreign policies are more of a threat to EU unity than are strong national policies. Here lies an important postcrisis challenge: European governments must avoid drifting toward a bean-counting approach to international policy. The logic has been that cutting back foreign policy resources is beneficial as it saves money, when such resources were always recognized as necessary to underpin European prosperity. The National Intelligence Council reasons that an inward turn by the EU and United States would be one of the steps most likely to risk worst-case scenarios of global conflict up to 2030.[32]

Henceforth, a different metric of power will be required: not so much the ability to obtain a certain definitive solution through sole agency, but rather the ability to influence global events that at least tempers risk. Europeans still need to make a huge change of perception, from very recently being asked to support India and China as poor states to now being concerned over their power. The EU will need to recast its notions of power. Degrees of power cannot be measured in mechanistically relative terms as in the nineteenth century. In the future world order, influence will not equate with structural weight. It is something to celebrate, not fear, if positive-sum solutions to global problems come from non-Western sources. The EU's aim must be to ensure such outcomes, rather than to preserve the traditional measures of its own power per se. At the very least, the EU will need a "smart" way of absorbing others' power.

While the eurozone crisis has prompted a reassessment of external EU policies, it has not yet generated a clear narrative of the unity required to deal with the postcrisis order—of the kind the Cecchini Report provided in kick-starting the single market program in the mid-1990s, by identifying concrete benefits and the costs of non-unity.[33] Such an exercise in setting common guidelines may help provide some of the glue necessary to preventing a two-speed Europe from rupturing foreign policy cooperation—such a risk being a significant spillover legacy from the crisis to external policies.

Many insist that the economic crisis renders investment in foreign policies of lower importance. Some in the corridors of power even mutter about an impending "end of foreign policy." Quite the opposite is required. Self-absorption cannot extirpate the ravages of crisis. An initial requirement is for a clear definition of geostrategic principles. Good geostrategy must eschew both too much of the one-idea hedgehog and too much of the flitting fox. It is unsustainable for the EU to think it can bask in postmodernism within Europe while guarding such a supposed Kantian paradise through realist bargaining outside its borders. This distinction must look increasingly untenable when the barriers between inside and outside are today so porous, and when at present internal crisis *is* the EU's external image. Far more internal and external innovation is required for the EU to meet the scale of the postcrisis challenge. Less unquestioning Monnet, more Sartre's motif that "existence precedes essence": the EU must move beyond its long-supposed intrinsic rationales. It must adapt, strive, flow, and find its purpose anew.

NOTES

CHAPTER 1

1. Quoted from T. S. Eliot, "Little Gidding," Four Quartets, in *T.S. Eliot Collected Poems 1909–1962* (London: Harcourt, 1963), 202.

2. Alfred Tennyson, "Ulysses," in *The Oxford Book of English Verse,* ed. C. Ricks (Oxford: Oxford University Press, 1999), 425.

3. William Blake, "Europe: A Prophecy," in *William Blake Complete Illuminated Poems* (London: Thames and Hudson, 1984).

CHAPTER 2

1. Sebastian Dullien, "Reinventing Europe: Explaining the Fiscal Compact," ECFR Comment, European Council on Foreign Relations, May 1, 2012, http://ecfr.eu/content/entry/commentary_reinventing_europe_explaining_the_fiscal_compact.

2. Arne Heise and Hanna Lierse, "Budget Consolidation and the European Social Model: The Effects of European Austerity Programmes on Social Security Systems," International Policy Analysis, Friedrich Ebert Stiftung, 2011.

3. Bill Emmott, *Good Italy, Bad Italy* (New Haven, Conn.: Yale University Press, 2012).

4. Sebastian Mallaby, "Europe's Optional Crisis," *Foreign Affairs* 91 (2012): 6–10.

5. Martin Wolf, "A New Form of European Union," *Financial Times*, June 12, 2012.

6. Indermit Gill and Martin Raiser, *Golden Growth: Restoring the Lustre of the European Economic Model* (Washington, D.C.: World Bank, 2010); Eurostat, Eurostat database, 2013.

7. Gregory Jackson and Richard Deeg, "The Long-Term Trajectories of Institutional Change in European Capitalism," *Journal of European Public Policy* 19, no. 8 (2012): 1109–24.

8. Alberto Alesina and Francesco Giavazzi, *The Future of Europe: Reform or Decline* (Cambridge, Mass.: MIT Press, 2008), 17.

9. Steven Hill, "Sustainable Good Society: Why the European Way Is Still the Best Hope in an Insecure Age," *Social Europe Journal*, November 21, 2011.

10. Anatole Kaltelsky, *Capitalism 4.0* (London: Public Affairs, 2010).

11. Joseph Stiglitz, *Freefall: Free Markets and the Sinking of the Global Economy* (London: Penguin, 2010), 301; Robert Skidelsky, "The Future of Globalisation in the Light of the Economic Collapse of 2008," paper presented at the International Institute for Strategic Studies, March 23, 2012.

12. "Big Five UK Banks Rue 'Dire Year' as 11 Billion Pounds of Fines Erase Profit Gains," *Guardian*, March 25, 2013.

13. Daniela Schwarzer, "Crisis and Reform in the Euro Area," *Current History*, March 2013.

14. C. Fred Bergsten, "Why the Euro Will Survive," *Foreign Affairs* 91, no. 5 (2012): 19.

15. Claudia Beyer et al., *Economy and Labour Markets in Europe*, Working Paper, Allianz Research, November 2012.

16. Roger Altman, "The Fall and Rise of the West," *Foreign Affairs* 92, no. 1 (2013): 8–14.

17. Ruchir Sharma, *Breakout Nations* (New York: Norton, 2013).

18. "Briefing: European Entrepreneurs," *Economist*, July 28, 2012.

19. Eurostat, *EU Budget 2012 in Figures* (Brussels: Eurostat, 2013).

20. Eurostat, *Europe 2020 Strategy: Toward a Smarter, Greener and More Inclusive EU Economy*, Eurostat Paper 39, 2012, 3.

21. "France Unveils €20 Billion in Business Tax Breaks to Boost Ailing Economy," France24, November 8, 2012, www.france24.com/en/20121106-france-economy-competitiveness-euro-bank-unveils-%E2%82%AC20-billion-tax-break-boost-industry.

22. Attila Marján, *Europe's Destiny: The Old Lady and the Bull* (Baltimore, Md.: Johns Hopkins University Press, 2010), 84–87.

23. Gill and Raiser, *Golden Growth*, 16.

24. European Commission, *Global Europe 2050* (Brussels: European Commission, 2012), 131.

25. Nicholas Crafts, "Saving the Eurozone: Is a 'Real' Marshall Plan the Answer?" Chatham House Working Paper, June 2012, www.chathamhouse.org/sites/default/files/public/Research/International%20Economics/0612bp_crafts.pdf.

26. Paul de Grauwe, George Magnus, Thomas Mayer, and Holger Schmeding, *The Future of Europe's Economy: Disaster or Deliverance?* (London: Centre for European Reform, September 2013).

27. Cesar Molinas, *Que hacer con Espana?* (Barcelona: Ediciones Destino, 2013).

28. Simon Tilford, *Europe Places Too Much Faith in Supply-Side Policies*, Centre for European Reform, January 18, 2013.

29. Nouriel Roubini, "The Eurzone's Calm Before the Storm," Project Syndicate, October 28, 2013; Wolfgang Munchau, "Optimsim About an End to the Euro Crisis Is Wrong," *Financial Times*, October 27, 2013.

30. Roger Liddle, "The Political Economy of the Single Market," in *The Delphic Oracle on Europe: Is There a Future for the European Union?* eds. Loukas Tsoukalis and Janis A. Emmanouilidis (Oxford: Oxford University Press, 2011), 115–16.

31. Gill and Raiser, *Golden Growth*, 18, 22, and 27.

32. Mark Leonard and Jan Zielonka, "A Europe of Incentives," ECFR Policy Brief, June 2012.

33. Anthony Giddens, *Europe in the Global Age* (Cambridge: Polity Press, 2007), 27.

34. Philip Cerny, *Rethinking World Politics: A Theory of Transnational Neopluralism* (Oxford: Oxford University Press, 2010), chapter 12, 266.

35. Tim Jackson, *Prosperity Without Growth* (London: Earthscan, 2009); Dieter Helm, "Green Growth: Opportunities, Challenges and Costs," in *The Delphic Oracle*, eds. Tsoukalis and Emmanouilidis.

36. Karl Aiginger, Olaf Cramme, Stefan Ederer, Roger Liddle, and Renaud Thillaye, "Reconciling the Short and the Long Run: Governance Reforms to the Crisis and Beyond," Policy Brief 1, Welfare, Wealth, Work Project, 2012.

37. John Gray, "A Point of View: What Would Keynes Do?" BBC News, July 21, 2012, www.bbc.co.uk/news/magazine-18923542.

38. Colin Crouch, *The Strange Non-Death of Neo-Liberalism* (Cambridge: Polity Press, 2011).

39. Thierry Chopin, Jean-Francois Jamet, and Francois-Xavier Priollaud, "A Political Union for Europe," Policy Paper 252, Fondation Robert Schuman, 2012.

40. Wolfgang Munchau, "Euro Crisis Will Last for Twenty Years," *Financial Times*, July 9, 2012.

41. Steven Kramer, "The Return of History in Europe," *Washington Quarterly*, Fall 2012.

42. European Commission, *Global Europe 2050*, 30, 136.

43. Salvatore Aloisio, Giorgio Grimaldi, Umberto Morelli, and Antonio Padoa-Schioppa, "The European Citizens' Initiative: Challenges and Perspectives," in *Democracy in the European Union After the Lisbon Treaty*, ed. R. Matarazzo (Rome: IAI, 2011).

44. Hugo Brady, *Time for a European Civil Liberties Union?* (London: Centre for European Reform Insight, September 2012).

45. Mary Kaldor and Sabine Selchow, *The Bubbling Up of Subterranean Politics in Europe* (London: LSE Civil Society and Human Security Unit, 2012), 18–19 and 24.

46. João Carlos Espada, "The Sources of Extremism," *Journal of Democracy* 23, no. 4 (2012): 16–23.

47. Sebastian Dullien and José Ignacio Torreblanca, "What Is Political Union?" ECFR Policy Brief, 2012.

48. Vivien Schmidt, *Democracy in Europe: The EU and National Politics* (Oxford: Oxford University Press, 2006).

49. Matteo Garavoglia, *Democracy in Europe: Politicising Champions for the European Public Sphere*, IAI Working Paper 11/14, Istituto Affari Internazionali, 2011.

50. Slavoj Zizek, *The Year of Dreaming Dangerously* (London: Verso, 2012), 12, 34.

51. Ivan Krastev, *In Mistrust We Trust* (Ted Books, 2013).

52. Jürgen Habermas, *The Crisis of the European Union* (Cambridge: Polity Press, 2012); Ulrich Beck and Edgar Grande, "Cosmopolitanism: Europe's Way Out of Crisis," *European Journal of Social Theory* 10/1 (2007): 67–85; John Dryzek, *Global Deliberative Politics* (Cambridge: Polity Press, 2006); Larry Siedentop, *Democracy in Europe* (London: Penguin, 2000); Tony Judt, *A Grand Illusion: An Essay on Europe* (New York: NYU Press, 2011); Kalypso Nicolaidis, "Sustainable Integration: Toward EU 2.0?" *Journal of Common Market Studies Annual Review* 48 (2010): 21–54; Frank Schimmelfennig, "The Normative Origins of Democracy in the European Union: Toward a Transformational Theory of Democratisation," (Working Paper 39) National Centre of Competence in Research, Switzerland, 2009; Brendan Simms, "Toward a Mighty Union: How to Create a Democratic European Superpower," *International Affairs* 88, no. 1 (2012): 49–62; Owen Parker, *Cosmopolitan Government in Europe* (London: Routledge, 2012), 124.

53. Nicole Bolleyer and Christine Reh, "EU Legitimacy Revisited: The Normative Foundations of a Multilevel Polity," *Journal of European Public Policy* 19, no. 4 (2012): 472–90.

54. Thomas Risse, *A Community of Europeans? Transnational Identities and Public Spheres* (Ithaca, N.Y.: Cornell University Press), 2010; J. McCormick, *Europeanism* (Oxford: Oxford University Press, 2010).

55. Giandomenico Majone, "The Traditional One-Size-Fits-All Approach to European Integration Is Obsolete," interview, Verfassungsblog, February 13, 2013; Giandomenico Majone, "Monetary Union and the Politicisation of Europe," keynote speech at the Euroacademia International Conference, Vienna, December 2011.

56. Mark Mazower, "What Remains: On the European Union," *Nation*, September 5, 2012.

57. Andrew Moravcsik, "Europe After the Crisis: How to Sustain a Common Currency," *Foreign Affairs*, May/June 2012, 67. Also, see his presentation at the annual conference of the Central European University, May 24, 2011.

58. Charles Grant, "Nothing to Celebrate," *Foreign Policy*, January 4, 2012.

59. Ulrich Beck, "Créons une Europe des Citoyens!" *Le Monde,* December 26, 2011, www.lemonde.fr/idees/article/2011/12/26/creons-une-europe-des-citoyens_1622792_3232.html.

60. Ulrich Beck, *German Europe* (Cambridge: Polity Press, 2013), 40, 43, and 64.

61. George Soros, "La Tragedia Europea," *El Pais*, September 12, 2012.

62. "Germany: The Reluctant Hegemon," *Economist Special Report*, June 2013.

63. David Marsh, *The Euro: The Battle for the New Global Currency* (New Haven, Conn.: Yale University Press, 2011), 288–93.

64. Philip Stephens, "Europe's Return to Westphalia," *Financial Times*, June 23, 2011.

65. Loukas Tsoukalis, "The Delphic Oracle on Europe," in *The Delphic Oracle*, eds. Tsoukalis and Emmanouilidis, 212.

66. Timothy Garton Ash, "Fear May Well Save the Euro. Now for the Politics of Hope," *Guardian*, January 25, 2012.

67. Ulrich Speck, "Why Germany Is Not Becoming Europe's Hegemon," Fride Policy Brief, April 2012.

68. Günter Grass, *My Century* (London: Houghton, 1999).

69. Josef Janning, "Europe: Germany's Dilemma," European Policy Centre, Policy Brief, December 2011, 3.

70. Mark Leonard, Jan Zielonka, and Nicolas Walton, "Introduction," in *The New Political Geography of Europe*, eds. Jan Zielonka and Nicolas Walton (London: European Council on Foreign Relations, 2013), 6.

71. Joel Shenton, "UK Defence Secretary to Back German Military Reform," PublicServiceEurope.com, May 2, 2012, www.publicserviceeurope.com/article/1880/uk-defence-secretary-to-back-german-military-reform.

72. Daniela Schwarzer and Kai-Olaf Lang, "The Myth of German Hegemony," *Foreign Affairs*, October 2012.

73. Judy Dempsey, "Merkel's Unfinished Business: Why Germany Needs to Act Strategically," Carnegie Paper, Carnegie Europe, September 2013.

74. Daniela Schwarzer and Guntram B. Wolff, "Memo to Merkel: Post-Election Germany and Europe," Bruegel Policy Brief, September 24, 2013, www.bruegel.org/download/parent/794-memo-to-merkel-post-election-germany-and-europe/file/1681-memo-to-merkel-post-election-germany-and-europe.

75. *New Power, New Responsibility: Elements of a German Foreign and Security Policy for a Changing World* (Berlin: German Marshall Fund and Stiftung Wissenschaft und Politik, 2013), 8.

76. Josef Joffe, "The Case for Muddling Through," *Europe's World* (Spring 2012): 78–82.

77. R. Daniel Kelemen, "Europe's New Normal," *Foreign Affairs*, May 17, 2012.

78. Pawel Swieboda, "Europe From Scratch," Demos Europa Policy Paper, February 2012.

CHAPTER 3

1. Niall Ferguson, *The Ascent of Money: A Financial History of the World* (London: Penguin, 2009).

2. World Trade Organization, "Trade Figures 2013" and "Trade Figures 2007" 13.

3. Dan Steinbock, "Europe's New Challenge: Eroding Foreign Investment," *European Observer*, September 26, 2013.

4. Guido Westerwelle, "Economic Success Is Also Good News for Foreign Policy," speech to the 2nd German Congress of Global Market Leaders, February 2012.

5. Joseph Stiglitz, *Freefall: Free Markets and the Sinking of the Global Economy* (London: Penguin, 2010), 190–91, 225.

6. Institute of International Finance, "Capital Flows to Emerging Market Economies," Research Note, October 13, 2012.

7. Tomas Valasek, *Surviving Austerity: The Case for a New Approach to EU Military Collaboration* (London: Centre for European Reform, 2011).

8. International Institute for Strategic Studies, *Military Balance 2012* (London: IISS, 2013).

9. European Commission, *Annual Report 2013 on the European Union's Development and External Assistance Policies and Their Implementation in 2012*, SWD 307final (August 23, 2013), http://ec.europa.eu/europeaid/multimedia/publications/documents/annual-reports/europeaid_annual_report_2013_highlights_en.pdf.

10. OECD DAC statistics database.

11. "Europe Entering Age of 'Aid Austerity,'" EUObserver, April 4, 2012, http://euobserver.com/foreign/115801.

12. Richard Gowan, "Is the G20 Bad for the EU?" *Politica Exterior* 44, November 2011.

13. Justin Vaïsse, Hans Kundnani, et al., *European Foreign Policy Scorecard 2012* (London: European Council on Foreign Relations, 2012), 10–11.

14. Chad Damro, "Market Power Europe: EU Externalisation and Market-Related Policies," Mercury project, E-Paper 5, 2010.

15. AUGUR project on *Challenges for Europe in the World on 2030*, Report from Work package 8, prepared by the Tiger Group of Kozminski University, 2011.

16. Daniel Thomas, "Still Punching Below Its Weight? Coherence and Effectiveness in European Union Foreign Policy," *Journal of Common Market Studies* 50, no. 3 (2012): 457–74.

17. Eric Helleiner and Stefano Pagliari, "The End of an Era in International Financial Regulation? A Postcrisis Research Agenda," *International Organization* 65 (Winter 2011): 169–200. See also the *Warwick Commission* for similar arguments.

18. Giovanni Grevi, "Why Strategic Partnerships Matter," Fride Working Paper, 2012.

19. Richard Whitman and Annemarie Rodt, "EU-Brazil Relations: A Strategic Partnership?" *European Foreign Affairs Review* 17, no. 1 (2012): 27–44.

20. "Membership: Currency Crisis Exacerbates 'Enlargement Fatigue,'" *Financial Times*, May 8, 2012.

21. Ulrich Krotz and Richard Maher, "International Relations Theory and the Rise of European Foreign and Security Policy," *World Politics* 63, no. 3 (2011): 548–79, 571.

22. Kalypso Nicolaidis, "Toward Sustainable Integration," Open Democracy, July 12, 2010.

23. Jürgen Habermas and Jacques Derrida, "February 15, or What Binds Europe Together: A Plea for a Common European Foreign Policy," *Constellations* 10, no. 3 (2003).

24. Martin Feldstein, "EMU and International Conflict," *Foreign Affairs*, November–December, 1997.

25. Hugo Dixon, "Can Europe's Divided House Stand?" *Foreign Affairs*, November–December 2011.

26. Charles Kupchan, "Centrifugal Europe," *Survival* 54, no. 1 (February 2012): 111–18.

27. Jean Pisani-Ferry, *How to Stop Fragmentation of the Eurozone* (Brussels: Bruegel, 2011).

28. Charlemagne, "Wake Up, Euro Zone," *Economist*, October 22, 2011, 34.

29. David Marquand, *The End of the West: The Once and Future Europe* (Princeton, N.J.: Princeton University Press, 2011).

30. Joschka Fischer, "Provincial Europe," Project Syndicate, October 31, 2012.

31. Stefan Lehne, "A More Ambitious Europe?" *European Voice*, September 20, 2012.

32. Stefan Lehne, *The Big Three in EU Foreign Policy*, Carnegie Paper, Carnegie Europe, 2012.

33. Gunther Hellmann, "Normatively Disarmed, But Self-Confident," *Internationale Politik* 3 (2011): 45–51.

34. Thans Dokos, "Who Lost Greece? The Geopolitical Consequences of the Greek Crisis," ELIAMEP Policy Paper 18, 2012.

35. Sebastian Rosato, "Europe's Troubles: Power Politics and the State of the European Project," *International Security* 35, no. 4 (2011): 45–86.

36. Stephan Keukeleire and Hans Bruyninckx, "The European Union, the BRICs and the Emerging New World Order," in *International Relations and the European Union*, 2nd edition, eds. Christopher Hill and Michael Smith (Oxford: Oxford University Press, 2012), 392.

37. Luuk van Middelaar, *Le Passage à l'Europe: Histoire d'un Commencement* (Paris: Éditions Gallimard, 2012), 11–13.

38. Loukas Tsoukalis, "The JCMS Annual Lecture: The Shattering of Illusion—And What Next?" *Journal of Common Market Studies Annual Review 2011* 49 (2012): 19–44.

39. Richard Rosecrance, Reinventing Europe blog post, European Council on Foreign Relations, January 23, 2012, www.ecfr.eu/blog/entry/reinventing_europe_richard_rosecrance.

40. José Manuel Barroso, "EU-India: A Strategic Relationship in an Evolving World," speech, Mumbai, February 13, 2012.

41. "Preparing the December 2013 European Council on Security and Defence Interim Report by the High Representative," July 24, 2013, http://eeas.europa.eu/library/publications/2013/24072013_hr_interim_report_en.pdf.

42. *Towards a European Global Strategy: Securing European Influence in a Changing World*, May 28, 2013, www.europeanglobalstrategy.eu/Files.aspx?f_id=91692.

43. Ulrich Krotz, Richard Maher, et al., "Debating the Sources and Prospects of European Integration," *International Security* 37, no. 1 (2012): 178–99.

44. Thomas Wright, "What If Europe Fails?" *Washington Quarterly* 35, no. 3 (2012): 23–41.

45. Andrew Cottey, *Security in 21st Century Europe*, 2nd edition (Basingstoke: Palgrave, 2012), chapter 10.

46. Alessandro Marrone, *Defence Spending in Europe in Light of the Economic Crisis*, Rome, Istituto Affari Internazionali Working Paper 12/27, October 2012.

47. "NATO: Ready, Robust, Rebalanced," Carnegie Europe event transcript, September 19, 2013, http://carnegieendowment.org/files/2013-09-19_NATO.pdf.

48. Anand Menon, *Europe: The State of the Union* (London: Atlantic Books, 2008).

49. Michael Leigh, "Is a Two-Speed Europe the Solution?" EuroFuture Project Paper, German Marshall Fund of the United States, February 2012.

50. Jean-Claude Piris, *The Future of Europe: Towards a Two-Speed Europe* (Cambridge: Cambridge University Press, 2012).

51. Dominique Moïsi, "Ten Reasons for Europe," *European Voice*, May 24, 2012, 12.

52. Mario Teló, Reinventing Europe blog post, February 23, 2012, http://ecfr.eu/blog/entry/reinventing_europe_mario_telo.

53. Mario Teló, "Introduction," in *The European Union and Global Governance*, ed. Mario Teló (London: Routledge, 2009).

54. Johan Eriksson, "Survival of the Fittest, Not the Strongest: Why the EU Will Prevail in the Global Power Game," Swedish Institute for International Affairs Brief 17, 2012.

55. Pawel Swieboda, *Europe From Scratch,* Demos Europa Policy Paper, February 2012, 7.

56. Harold James, Reinventing Europe blog post, January 18, 2012, http://ecfr.eu/blog/entry/reinventing_europe_harold_james.

57. Interview for ISN Network, April 23, 2012.

58. Robert Kagan, "How the Fiscal Crisis Puts National Security at Risk," *Washington Post*, November 12, 2012.

CHAPTER 4

1. Mark Thirwell, "The Return of Geo-Economics: Globalisation and National Security," Commentary, Lowy Institute for International Policy, 2010, www.lowyinstitute.org/files/pubfiles/Thirlwell%2C_The_return_of_geo-economics_web_and_print.pdf.

2. Maaike Okano-Heijmans, "Power Shift: Economic Realism and Economic Diplomacy on the Rise," in *Power in the 21st Century*, eds. Enrico Fels et al. (Heidelberg: Springer, 2012).

3. Eurasia Group, *Top Risks 2012*, New York, 2012, http://eurasiagroup.net/pages/top-risks-2012.

4. Parag Khanna, "Introductory Thoughts," paper delivered at the International Institute for Strategic Studies, March 23, 2012.

5. Stephen D. King, *Losing Control: The Emerging Threats to Western Prosperity* (New Haven, Conn.: Yale University Press, 2011), 232.

6. Dambisa Moyo, *How the West Was Lost: Fifty Years of Economic Folly—and the Stark Choices Ahead* (London: Penguin, 2012), 137, 152–53.

7. Parag Khanna, "Europe Needs a Truly Global Action Plan for 2020," in *Strategic Europe*, ed. Jan Techau (Brussels: Carnegie Europe, 2012), 116.

8. Robert Skidelsky, *The Future of Globalisation in the Light of the Economic Collapse of 2008*, paper delivered at the International Institute for Strategic Studies, March 23, 2012.

9. Alex Callinicos, *Bonfire of Illusions* (Cambridge: Polity Press, 2010).

10. Herman Van Rompuy, "Europe's Political and Economic Challenges in a Changing World," Special Winston Churchill Lecture, Zurich, November 9, 2011.

11. Richard Rosencrance, *The Rise of the Trading State: Commerce and Conquest in the Modern World* (London: Basic Books, 1986).

12. Andreas Dür and Manfred Elsig, "Principals, Agents, and the European Union's Foreign Economic Policies," *Journal of European Public Policy* 18, no. 3 (2011): 323–38.

13. Stephen Woolcock, *European Union Economic Diplomacy* (Farnham: Ashgate, 2012), 20, 43, 67, 79–80.

14. Peter Gumbel, "Is France Closing for Business?" Great Debate blog, Reuters, May 23, 2012, http://blogs.reuters.com/great-debate/2012/05/23/is-france-closing-for-business.

15. Lord Heseltine, *No Stone Unturned: In Pursuit of Growth* (London, Department for Business, Innovation and Skills, 2012).

16. Karel De Gucht, "EU-Asian Cooperation in an Era of Transformation," speech, Hong Kong, February 16, 2012.

17. European Parliament, *Protectionism in the G20 2012*, Policy Briefing, EP Directorate General for External Relations of the EU Department, 2011/293, 2011, 23.

18. "Débâcle: The 11th GTA Report on Protectionism," Centre for Economic Policy Research, June 2012, www.globaltradealert.org/sites/default/files/GTA11_0.pdf.

19. Max Nisen, "Trade War: How 12 Major Economies Have Closed Up Since the Crisis," *Business Insider*, June 18, 2012, www.businessinsider.com/global-protectionism- 2012-6?op=1.

20. Patrick Messerlin, "How the Rich OECD Nations Should Handle the Emerging Giants," *Europe's World* (Spring 2010): 15; Fredrik Erixson and Razeen Sally, *Trade, Globalisation and Emerging Protectionism Since the Crisis*, ECIPE Working Paper 2, 2010, 8, 12.

21. Overseas Development Institute, *The Next Decade of EU Trade Policy*, July 2012.

22. European Parliament, *Protectionism in the G20*, 14.

23. Joseph Stiglitz, *Freefall: Free Markets and the Sinking of the Global Economy* (London: Penguin, 2010), 213.

24. "Boxed In: International Trade," *Economist*, September 8, 2012.

25. "Putting Foreign Trade Back in the Service of Employment—Excerpts From the Communiqué Issued Following the Council of Ministers' Meeting," September 12, 2012, www.diplomatie.gouv.fr/en/french-foreign-policy-1/economic-diplomacy/trade-and-global-issues/article/putting-foreign-trade-back-in-the.

26. Bernd von Münchow-Pohl, "EU Relations With China and India: Courting the Dragon, Wooing the Elephant," Carnegie Paper, Carnegie Endowment for International Peace, 2012.

27. European Commission, *A Stronger European Industry for Growth and Economic Recovery*, Brussels, COM 582, October 2012.

28. Charlemagne, "Unfree Trade," *Economist*, March 24, 2012.

29. Simon J. Everett, ed., *Débâcle: The 11th G7 Report on Protectionism* (London: Centre for Economic Policy Research, 2012), chapter 5.

30. Ben Clift and Cornelia Woll, "Economic Patriotism: Reinventing Control Over Open Markets," *Journal of European Public Policy* 19, no. 3 (2012): 307–23. In this same special edition, for an excellent overview of EU "market construction," see Ben Rosamond, "Supranational Governance as Economic Patriotism? The European Union, Legitimacy and the Reconstruction of State Space," *Journal of European Public Policy* 19, no. 3.

31. Okano-Heijmans, "Power Shift."

32. Hans Kundnani, "Germany as a Geo-Economic Power," *Washington Quarterly*, Summer 2011.

33. Kristina Kausch, "A Geo-Economic Germany?" in *Challenges for European Foreign Policy in 2012: What Kind of Geo-Economic Europe?* eds. Richard Youngs and Ana Martiningui (Madrid: Fride, 2011), 47.

34. Hans Kundnani and Jonas Parello-Plesner, "China and Germany: Why the Emerging Special Relationship Matters for Europe," ECFR Policy Brief, May 2012.

35. "Europe Needs Unity, Economic Success for Global Say: Merkel," Agence France-Presse, September 18, 2012.

36. UKTI, *Britain: Open for Business*, 2012, 11; UK Department for Business Innovation and Skills, "International Trade and Investment: The Economic Rationale for Government Support," BIS Economic Paper 13, 2011.

37. HMG, *Trade and Investment for Growth* (London: BIS, 2011).

38. Foreign and Commonwealth Office, *Charter for Business*, 2010.

39. Philip Stephens, "UK Foreign Policy Should Be Realist," *Financial Times*, September 21, 2012.

40. Anna Walker, "The UK and Central Asia," EUCAM Policy Brief, Fride, July 2012.

41. Lord Howell, Foreign Office minister, "UK Relations With the GCC Region: A Broadening Partnership," speech, GCC and the City Conference, June 20, 2012.

42. David Rennie, *The Continent or the Open Sea: Does Britain Have a European Future?* (London: Centre for European Reform, 2012), 63.

43. Bagehot, "Cutty Sark Britain," *Economist*, April 12, 2012, www.economist.com/blogs/bagehot/2012/04/britain-and-eu.

44. See the website of the Italian Foreign Ministry, www.esteri.it/MAE/IT/Ministero/Servizi/Imprese/DiplomaziaEconomica.

45. Claus Grube, "The International Situation and Danish Foreign Policy in 2011," in *Danish Foreign Policy Yearbook 2012*, Danish Institute for International Studies, 24.

46. Huub Ruël and Lennart Zuidema, "The Effectiveness of Commercial Diplomacy: A Survey Among Dutch Embassies and Consulates," Clingendael Discussion Paper no. 123, March 2012.

47. Mark Rutte, Policy Statement, "Building Bridges," November 13, 2012, www.government.nl/government/policy-statement.

48. Demos Europa, *Poland and the World in 2030*, www.demoseuropa.eu/index.php?option=com_content&view=article&id=1098%3Apolska-2030-qglobalizacja-polskiej-polityki-zagranicznej-i-europejskiejq&catid=137%3A2012events&Itemid=160&lang=en.

49. Okano-Heijmans, "Power Shift."

50. Kausch, "A Geo-Economic Germany?" 49.

51. Ruël and Zuidema, "The Effectiveness of Commercial Diplomacy," 24.

52. Daniela Vincenti, "Thumann: Careful About Bashing China," interview with Jürgen R. Thumann, Euractiv, September 21, 2012, www.euractiv.com/global-europe/thumannthum-careful-bashing-chin-interview-514935.

53. Jean-Pierre Lehmann, "Absurd EU-Japan Trade Plan Underlines Doha's Failure," *Financial Times*, July 20, 2012.

54. Joshua Cooper Ramo, *The Age of the Unthinkable* (London: Little Brown, 2009); Parag Khanna, *How to Rule the World* (New York: Random House, 2011).

55. Ian Bremmer, *The End of the Free Market* (London: Portfolio Penguin, 2011).

56. Ana Echagüe, "Commercial Diplomacy in Europe: The Hunt for Growth," Fride Policy Brief, 2012.

57. Jonas Parello-Plessner, "Germany and China's New Entente Commerciale," *E!Sharp*, June 29, 2011.

58. Katinka Barysch, "The EU and Russia: All Smiles and No Action?" Centre for European Reform Policy Brief, April 2011.

59. Andrew Erdmann, "Managing Economic, Political and Geopolitical Uncertainty in the Era of Geo-Economics," paper delivered at the International Institute for Strategic Studies, March 23, 2012.

60. Attila Marján, *Europe's Destiny: The Old Lady and the Bull* (Baltimore, Md.: Johns Hopkins University Press, 2010).

61. Grube, "The International Situation," 28.

CHAPTER 5

1. *Project Europe 2030: Challenges and Opportunities*, Reflection Group on the Future of the EU 2030, 2010, 13.

2. Shada Islam, "Europe and the Asian Century," Friends of Europe Policy Briefing, June 2011, 3.

3. Karine Lisbonne-de Vergeron, *Chinese and Indian Views of Europe since the Crisis - New Perspectives from the Emerging Asian Giants* (French) (Paris: Fondation Robert Schuman, 2012).

4. Bertrand de Crombrugghe, "The Value of the Asia-Europe Meeting," *Studia Diplomatica* 64, no. 3 (2011): 99, 109–27.

5. European Union, "EU-Asia Factsheet," 2012.

6. Reported in *Global Europe*, May 4, 2012.

7. William Hague, "An Important Year for UK-China Relations," speech at the China Business summit, July 27, 2012.

8. Jean-Yves Le Drian, speech to IISS Asia Security Summit, Singapore, June 2012.

9. "ASEM: Still Relevant After All These Years?" Friends of Europe Policy Briefing, September 2012.

10. Xuan Loc Doan, "Opportunities and Challenges in EU-ASEAN Trade Relations," EU-Asian Centre, July 2012.

11. Anne Pollet-Fort and Yeo Lay Hwee, "EU-Asian Trade Relations: Getting Through the Crisis," Fride Agora Asia-Europe Policy Brief 2, 2012.

12. "EU, China Leaders Agree to Disagree," Euractiv, September 21, 2012, www.euractiv.com/global-europe/eu-china-leaders-agree-disagree-news-514940.

13. European Commission, *Mid-Term Review of Regional Strategy for Asia 2007–2013*, 2010.

14. Yeo Lay Hwee, "Where Is ASEM Heading—Toward a Networked Approach to Global Governance?" in *Panorama: Asia and Europe: Moving Toward a Common Agenda*, ed. Wilhelm Hofmeister (Singapore: Konrad Adenauer Stiftung, 2011).

15. Evi Fitriani, "Asian Perceptions About the EU in the Asia-Europe Meeting (ASEM)," *Asia Europe Journal* 4, no. 9 (2011): 43–56.

16. Gungwu Wang, "The China Effect in Anxious Europe," *Asia Europe Journal* 10, no. 3 (2012): 335–40.

17. Arif H. Oegroseno, "Europe's Asian Awakening Still Lacks Real Clout," *Europe's World*, Autumn 2012.

18. May-Britt Stumbaum, "How Does Asia View the EU?" NFG Research Group, Working Paper 1, Free University of Berlin, 2012.

19. "Europe Must Do 'Real' Business," BBC News, February 7, 2012, www.bbc.co.uk/news/16930889.

20. Hans Timmer and Uri Dadush, *The Euro Crisis and Emerging Economies*, Carnegie Endowment for International Peace, 2011, http://carnegieendowment.org/2011/12/16/euro-crisis-and-emerging-economies/8kj6.

21. Nicola Casarini, "The European 'Pivot,'" EU-ISS Issue Alert, March 2013, 1, www.iss.europa.eu/publications/detail/article/the-european-pivot.

22. "Japan Weighs Purchase of First Eurozone Bailout Bonds," Euractiv, January 7, 2013, www.euractiv.com/euro-finance/japan-weighs-purchase-eurozone-b-news-516894.

23. Nicola Casarini, "The EU and China: Investing in a Troubled Partnership," in *Partners in Crisis: EU Strategic Partnerships and the Global Downturn*, eds. G. Grevi and T. Renard (Madrid: Fride, 2012).

24. Fraser Cameron, "Two Good Summits," EU-Asia Centre, February 2012, www.eu-asiacentre.eu/pub_details.php?pub_id=40.

25. "EU Sees Dramatic Surge in Investment From China," EUObserver, June 7, 2012, http://euobserver.com/china/116537.

26. Asian Development Bank, *How Can Asia Respond to Global Economic Crisis and Transformation?* (Manila: Asian Development Bank, 2012).

27. Ravi Balakrishnan, Sylwia Nowak, Sanjaya Panth, and Yiqun Wu, "Surging Capital Flows to Emerging Asia: Facts, Impacts and Responses," IMF Working Paper 130, 2012.

28. Fraser Cameron, "The EU Is Engaging Asia," *New Europe*, October 22, 2012.

29. J. W. Blankert, "ASEAN and the EU: Natural Partners," in *EU-ASEAN Relations in the 21st Century*, eds. Daniel Novotny and Clara Portela (London: Palgrave, 2012), 148.

30. Martin Jacques, *When China Rules the World*, 2nd edition (London: Penguin, 2012), 606–607.

31. Odd A. Westad, "China and Europe: Opportunities or Dangers?" in *Europe in the Asian Century*, LSE Ideas Special Report, October 2012, 18.

32. Hans Kundnani and Jonas Parello-Plesner, "China and Germany: Why the Emerging Special Relationship Matters for Europe," ECFR Policy Brief, May 2012, 8.

33. Jeremy Clegg and Hinrich Voos, "Chinese Overseas Direct Investment in the European Union," ECRAN Working Paper, 2012.

34. Brigid Gavin, *China's Expanding Foreign Investment in Europe: New Policy Challenges for the EU* (Brussels: European Institute for Asian Studies, 2012), 3.

35. European Council on Foreign Relations, *European Foreign Policy Scorecard 2013*, 28–29.

36. Gavin, *China's Expanding Foreign Investment in Europe*, 13.

37. Institute of International Finance, *Capital Flows to Emerging Market Economies*, 2012.

38. Isabella Massa, Jodie Keane, and Jane Kennan, *The Eurozone Crisis and Developing Countries* (London: ODI, 2012), 8, 39, 42. For similar evidence, see also Naoyuki Yoshino, "Global Imbalances and the Development of Capital Flows Among Asian Countries," *OECD Journal: Financial Market Trends*, issue 1, 2012.

39. Jean Pisani-Ferry, "China to the Rescue?" *Foreign Policy*, December 29, 2011.

40. George Magnus, *Asia's Fading Economic Miracle* (London: Centre for European Reform, 2013).

41. Eva Schilling, *When the Rising Dragon Sees Fading Stars: China's View of the European Union*, CEPS special report 73, 2012.

42. Nicola Casarini, "For China, the Euro Is a Safer Bet Than the Dollar," EU Institute for Security Studies Analysis, June 2012.

43. Miguel Otero-Iglesias, "China, the Euro and Reform of the International Monetary System," in *Brussels-Beijing: Changing the Game?* ed. Nicola Casarini, Report no. 14, EU Institute for Security Studies, 2013, 31.

44. Ruchir Sharma, *Breakout Nations: In Pursuit of the Next Economic Miracles* (New York: Norton, 2013), 18.

45. Chen Zhimin, "The Efficacy of Post-Lisbon Treaty EU External Actions and the China–EU Strategic Partnership," in *The EU's Foreign Policy: What Kind of Power and Diplomatic Action?* eds. Mario Teló and Frederik Ponjaert (Farnham: Ashgate, 2013).

46. Chen Zhimin, "Europe as a Global Player: A View from China," in *Perspectives: Review of International Affairs* 20, no. 2 (2012): 7–29.

47. See European Commission, DG Trade, "Statistics," http://ec.europa.eu/trade/policy/countries-and-regions/statistics/index_en.htm.

48. Thomas Kleine-Brockhoff, ed., *Weighing Europe: How Europe's Global Partners Assess Power and Influence of a Region in Crisis* (Washington, D.C.: German Marshall Fund of the United States, 2013).

49. John Armstrong, *The EU's Trade Policy and China: Cooperation in the Interest of Multilateralism?* Mercury Project, E-paper 21, 2012.

50. Fredrik Erixon, *Mercantilist Misperceptions: A Detente Strategy for EU-China Relations* (Brussels: European Centre for International Political Economy, 2012), 5.

51. Jonathan Holslag, "EU Should Stay Out of Security Matters in Asian Pacific," *European Voice*, July 4, 2012; Bernd von Münchow-Pohl, "EU Relations With China and India: Courting the Dragon, Wooing the Elephant," Carnegie Paper, Carnegie Endowment for International Peace, 2012; Jonathan Holslag, *Crowded, Connected and Contested: Security and Peace in the Eurasian Sea and What It Means for Europe* (Brussels: Brussels Institute of Contemporary China Studies, 2012).

52. EU External Action Service, *Guidelines on the EU's Foreign and Security Policy in East Asia*, June 2012.

53. Catherine Ashton, "Defending National Interests, Preventing Conflict," speech at the Shangri-La Dialogue, June 1, 2013, A291/13.

54. French Foreign Ministry, *France and Europe in Asia*, 2011.

55. Guido Westerwelle, *Europe at a Cross-Roads: The Sovereign Debt Crisis and Its Impact on Asia*, speech to the Asian Society in Hong Kong, August 31, 2012.

56. See the Italian Foreign Ministry website, www.esteri.it/MAE/IT/Politica_Estera/Aree_Geografiche/Asia.

57. David O'Sullivan, "Priorities for EU Diplomacy in East Asia," speech at the GRIPS Forum, Tokyo, February 12, 2013.

58. Jonas Parello-Plesner, "Europe's Mini-Pivot to Asia," *China-US Focus*, November 6, 2012, www.chinausfocus.com/foreign-policy/europes-mini-pivot-to-asia.

59. Yeo Lay Hwee, "The EU as a Security Actor in Southeast Asia," in *Panorama: Insights Into Asian and European Affairs: Security Politics in Asia and Europe*, ed. Wilhelm Hofmeister (Singapore: Konrad Adenauer Stiftung, 2010).

60. Naila Maier-Knapp, "The EU and Non-Traditional Security in South East Asia," in Novotny and Portela, *EU-ASEAN*, 39.

61. Jonas Parello-Plesner, "The EU as Asian Partner," *East Asian Forum*, July 12, 2012.

62. Constanze Stenzenmuller, "Asia to Europe: We Need to Discuss Our Relationship," GMF blog, June 6, 2012, http://blog.gmfus.org/2012/06/06/asia-to-europe-we-need-to-discuss-our-relationship.

63. Michito Tsuruoka, "Defining Europe's Strategic Interests in Asia: State of Things and Challenges Ahead," *Studia Diplomatica* 64, no. 3 (2011): 95–108.

64. Islam, *Europe and the Asian Century*.

65. Daniel Keohane, "The EU's Role in East Asian Security," in *Look East, Act East: Transatlantic Agendas in the Asia Pacific*, ed. Patryk Pawlak, EU Institute for Security Studies, Report 13, 2012.

66. Europe-Asia Policy Forum, *Final Report*, 2012.

CHAPTER 6

1. Gideon Rachman, *Zero-Sum World: Politics, Power and Prosperity After the Crash* (London: Atlantic Books, 2010); Paul Berman, *Terror and Liberalism* (London and New York: Norton, 2004); Stefano Casertano, "The Return of Cold War Logic," *European*, February 15, 2012, www.theeuropean-magazine.com/stefano-casertano--3/555-big-power-politics-in-the-middle-east; Mark Malloch-Brown, *Unfinished Global Revolution: The Road to International Cooperation* (New York: Penguin Press, 2011), 12; Amy Chua, *World on Fire: How Exporting Free Market Democracy Breeds Ethnic Hatred and Global Instability* (New York: Random House, 2004); Colin Elman and Michael Jensen, "Realisms," in *Security Studies: An Introduction*, 2nd ed., ed. Paul Williams (New York: Routledge, 2012).

2. Mark Mazower, *Governing the World: The History of an Idea* (London: Penguin, 2012).

3. Ian Bremmer, *Every Nation for Itself: Winners and Losers in a G-Zero World* (London: Portfolio Penguin, 2012).

4. Mark Leonard, "The Central Challenge to the Western Liberal Order Is the Rise of the Post-Colonial Superpowers (With American Support)," Global Trends 2030, May 31, 2012, http://gt2030.com/2012/05/30/the-central-challenge-to-the-western-liberal-order-is-the-rise-of-the-post-colonial-superpowers-with-american-support.

5. Charles Kupchan, *No One's World: The West, the Rising Rest, and the Coming Global Turn* (Oxford: Oxford University Press, 2012).

6. Martin Jacques, *When China Rules the World*, 2nd ed. (London: Penguin, 2012), 621–22.

7. Naazneen Barma, Ely Ratner, and Steven Weber, "The Mythical Liberal Order," *National Interest*, March-April 2013.

8. Nick Mabey, "Facing the Climate Security Threat: Why the Security Community Needs a 'Whole-of-Government' Response to Global Climate Change," GMF Policy Brief, November 2010, 2; Thomas Friedman, *Hot, Flat and Crowded: Why We Need a Green Revolution—And How It Can Renew America* (London: Penguin, 2009); James Lovelock, *The Vanishing Face of Gaia: A Final Warning* (London: Penguin, 2009).

9. Andrew Linklater, *The Transformation of Political Community* (Cambridge: Cambridge University Press, 1998); Richard Beardsworth, *Cosmopolitanism and International Relations Theory* (Cambridge: Polity Press, 2011).

10. Steven Webber and Bruce Jentleson, *The End of Arrogance: America in the Global Competition of Ideas* (Cambridge, Mass.: Harvard University Press, 2010), 104; Stephen Chan, *The End of Certainty: Toward a New Internationalism* (London: Zed, 2010).

11. Francis Fukuyama, *The Origins of Political Order* (New York: Ferrar, Straus, and Giroux, 2011); Ivan Krastev, "Paradoxes of the New Authoritarianism," *Journal of Democracy* 22, no. 2 (2011).

12. G. John Ikenberry, "The Future of the Liberal World Order: Internationalism After America," *Foreign Affairs*, May/June 2011; and G. John Ikenberry, *Liberal Leviathan* (Princeton, N.J.: Princeton University Press, 2011).

13. Moisés Naím, *The End of Power* (New York: Basic Books, 2013).

14. EU Institute for Security Studies, *Global Trends 2030: Citizens in an Interconnected and Polycentric World* (Paris: EUISS, 2012), http://europa.eu/espas/pdf/espas_report_ii_01_en.pdf.

15. United Nations Development Program, *Human Development Report 2013* (New York: UNDP, 2013).

16. Kishore Muhbubani, *The Great Convergence: Asia, the West and the Logic of One World* (New York: Public Affairs, 2013).

17. Mary Kaldor, Sabine Selchow, and Henrietta Moore, eds., *Global Civil Society 2012: Ten Years of Critical Reflection* (Basingstoke: Palgrave Macmillan, 2012).

18. David Held, *Cosmopolitanism: Ideals and Realities* (Cambridge: Polity Press, 2010).

19. Philip Cerny, *Rethinking World Politics: A Theory of Transnational Neo-Pluralism* (Oxford: Oxford University Press, 2010).

20. Ulrich Beck, *Cosmopolitan Vision* (Cambridge: Polity Press, 2006), 59.

21. Niall Ferguson, *Civilization: The West and the Rest* (London: Penguin, 2011).

22. Attila Marján, *Europe's Destiny: The Old Lady and the Bull* (Baltimore, Md.: Johns Hopkins University Press, 2010), 336.

23. Rebekka Friedman, Kevork Oskanian, and Ramon Pacheco Pardo, eds., *After Liberalism? The Future of Liberalism in International Relations* (London: Palgrave Macmillan, 2013).

24. Tim Dunne and Trine Flockhart, eds., *Liberal World Orders* (Oxford: Oxford University Press, 2013).

25. Shaun Breslin, "China's Emerging Global Role: Dissatisfied Responsible Great Power," *Politics* 30, no. 1 (2010): 52–62.

26. Charles Grant, *Russia, China and Global Governance* (London: Centre for European Reform, 2012).

27. Thomas Carothers and Richard Youngs, "Looking for Help: Will Rising Democracies Become International Democracy Supporters?" Carnegie Paper, Carnegie Endowment for International Peace, July 2011.

28. Tim Dunne, "The Liberal Order and the Modern Project," *Millennium* 38, no. 3 (2010): 535–43.

29. Michael Smith, "Beyond the Comfort Zone: Internal Crisis and Challenges in the EU's Response to Rising Powers," *International Affairs* 89 no. 3 (2013): 653–71.

30. Mercury Project, "Organised Multilateralism: The EU in Multilateral Fora," Policy Brief 4, 2012.

31. Joachim Krause and Natalino Ronzitti, eds., *The EU, the UN and Collective Security: Making Multilateralism Effective* (London: Routledge, 2012).

32. Fulvio Attinà, "EU and the Structure of Government of the Global Political System: The Case of Multilateral Security," paper delivered to the 22nd IPSA Conference, Madrid, July 2012.

33. Giovanni Grevi and Thomas Renard, eds., *Partners in Crisis: EU Strategic Partnerships and the Global Downturn* (Madrid: Fride, 2012).

34. David Held, *Models of Democracy* (Cambridge: Polity Press, 2006), 304.

35. John Ruggie, "Multilateralism: The Anatomy of an Institutional Form," *International Organization* 64, no. 3 (1992): 561–98.

36. Daniele Archibugi, *The Global Commonwealth of Citizens: Toward Cosmopolitan Democracy* (Princeton, N.J.: Princeton University Press, 2008); Hakan Altinay, "The Case for Global Civics," Brookings Institution, March 2010; World Economic Forum, "Everybody's Business: Strengthening International Cooperation in a More Interdependent World" (Geneva: World Economic Forum, 2010), 30, 144.

37. Andrew Cooper and Paola Subacchi, "Overview," in "Global Economic Governance in Transition," eds. Andrew Cooper and Paola Subacchi, *International Affairs* 86, no. 3, special edition (May 2010): 609.

38. OECD, *2012 DAC Report on Multilateral Aid* (Paris: Organization for Economic Cooperation and Development, 2012), 56.

39. Daniel Keohane, "Strategic Priorities for EU Defence Policy," Fride Policy Brief, February 2013, 2.

40. European External Action Service, *European External Action Service Review 2013*, 5, http://eeas.europa.eu/library/publications/2013/3/2013_eeas_review_en.pdf .

41. Frank Ledwidge, *Losing Small Wars* (New Haven, Conn.: Yale University Press, 2011).

42. "British Army Gears Up for Painful Challenge," *Financial Times*, July 6, 2012.

43. Julian Lindley-French, *Strategic Pretence or Strategic Defence?* GCSP Policy Paper 14, April 2011, 4.

44. "Flexing Its Muscles: As the Only Big Country in Europe That Is Increasing Defence Spending, Poland Wants More Say in NATO," *Economist*, August 17, 2013, 21.

45. Ulrich Speck, "Pacifism Unbound: Why Germany Limits EU Hard Power," Fride Policy Brief, May 2011, www.fride.org/publication/907/pacifism-unbound:-why-germany-limits-eu-hard-power.

46. Alessandro Colombo and Ettore Greco, "L'Italia e la trasformazione dello scenario internazionale," *IAI Documenti* 12, no. 3 (April 2012).

47. Doug Stokes and Richard Whitman, "Transatlantic Triage? European and UK 'Grand Strategy' After the U.S. Rebalance to Asia," *International Affairs* 89 no. 5 (2013): 1087–1107.

48. Michael E. Smith, "A Liberal Grand Strategy in a Realist World? Power, Purpose and the EU's Changing Global Role," *Journal of European Public Policy* 18, no. 2 (2011): 144–63.

49. Stefan Lehne, "The Role of Sanctions in EU Foreign Policy," Carnegie Endowment for International Peace, December 2012, http://carnegieendowment.org/2012/12/14/role-of-sanctions-in-eu-foreign-policy/etnv.

50. DFID, "Governance Portfolio Review," Department for International Development, July 2011, 4, 6.

51. Danida, "The Rights to a Better Life: Strategy for Denmark's Development Cooperation," 2011.

52. Netherlands Foreign Ministry, "Responsible for Freedom: Human Rights in Foreign Policy," 2011.

53. French Foreign Ministry, "Democratic Governance and Human Rights," 2010.

54. Tsveta Petrova, "The New Role of Central and Eastern Europe in International Democracy Support," Carnegie Paper, Carnegie Endowment for International Peace, June 2011.

55. EUStat, "EU Budget 2012 in Figures," 2012.

56. European Commission, "Instrument for Stability, 2011 Annual Report," Brussels, 2012.

57. External Action Service and European Commission, *Implementation of the Agenda for Action on Democracy Support in the EU's External Relations,* JOIN (2012) 28, October 2012, 4–5.

58. European Commission, "Increasing the Impact of EU Development Policy: An Agenda for Change," COM 637, 2011.

59. Council of the European Union, *Annual Report on Human Rights and Democracy in the World 2012*, 9431/13, May 13, 2013, 69–70 and 79, http://register.consilium.europa.eu/pdf/en/13/st09/st09431.en13.pdf.

60. European Commission, "The Roots of Democracy and Sustainable Development: Europe's Engagement With Civil Society in External Relations," COM 492, September 2012.

61. Sofía Sebastian, "Bosnia's Logjam," Fride Policy Brief, January 2013.

62. European Commission and High Representative, "European Neighbourhood Policy: Working Toward a Stronger Partnership," SWD 85, 2013.

63. Andrew Wilson, "The EU and Ukraine After the 2012 Election," European Council on Foreign Relations, 2012, 4, http://ecfr.eu/content/entry/the_eu_and_ukraine_after_the_2012_elections.

64. ECFR, *Scorecard 2012* (London: European Council on Foreign Relations, 2013), 44.

65. Dmitri Trenin, Maria Lipman, and Alexey Malashenko, "The End of an Era in EU-Russia Relations," Carnegie Paper, Carnegie Moscow Center, 2013.

66. Shada Islam and Patricia Diaz, "EU-Myanmar: Charting a Course for the Future," Friends of Europe Policy Brief, April 2013.

67. Mikael Mattlin, "Dead on Arrival: Normative EU Policy Toward China," *Asia Europe Journal* 10, no. 2 (2012): 181–98.

CHAPTER 7

1. Robert Kagan, *The World America Made* (New York: Vintage, 2013), 109–110.

2. Future of Europe Group, *Final Report of the Foreign Ministers of Austria, Belgium, Denmark, France, Italy, Germany, Luxembourg, the Netherlands, Poland, Portugal, and Spain*, September 17, 2012, www.statewatch.org/news/2012/sep/eu-future-of-europe-report.pdf.

3. Eberhard Sandschneider, *Der Erfolgreiche Abstieg Europas—Heute Macht Abgeben um Morgen zu Gewinnen* [Europe's Successful Descent—Giving Away Power Today in Order to Win Tomorrow] (Munich: Carl Hanser Verlag, 2011).

4. Joseph Nye, *The Future of Power* (New York: Public Affairs, 2011).

5. Albert Bressand, "Between Kant and Machiavelli: EU Foreign Policy Priorities in the 2010s," *International Affairs* 87, no. 1 (2011): 59–85, 61.

6. Walter Laqueur, *After the Fall: The End of the European Dream and the Decline of a Continent* (New York: St. Martin's Press, 2011).

7. Thomas Wright, "What If Europe Fails?" *Washington Quarterly* 35, no. 3 (2012): 23–41.

8. United Nations Development Program, *Human Development Report 2013*, 112–13, http://hdr.undp.org/en/reports/global/hdr2013/download.

9. Ulrich Beck and Edgar Grande, "Cosmopolitanism: Europe's Way Out of Crisis," *European Journal of Social Theory* 10, no. 1 (2007).

10. Susanne Gratius, "Brazil and the European Union: Between Balancing and Bandwagoning," Fride Working Paper, July 2012.

11. German Foreign Ministry, "Shaping Globalisation: Expanding Partnerships, Sharing Responsibilities," 2012.

12. Jean-François Rischard, *High Noon: 20 Global Problems, 20 Years to Solve Them* (New York: Basic Books, 2002).

13. Jolyon Howorth, "The EU as a Global Actor: Grand Strategy for a Global Grand Bargain?" *Journal of Common Market Studies* 48, no. 3 (2010): 455–74.

14. European Commission, "Global Europe 2050," 2012, 121.

15. Alex Vines, "The Effectiveness of UN and EU Sanctions: Lessons for the Twenty-First Century," *International Affairs* 88, no. 4 (2012): 867–77; Clara Portela, *European Union Sanctions and Foreign Policy: When and Why Do They Work?* (London: Routledge, 2010).

16. Anthony Giddens, *Turbulent and Mighty Continent: What Is the Future for Europe?* (Cambridge: Polity Press, 2013), 16.

17. Commission of the European Communities, *Taking Stock of the European Neighbourhood Policy*, COM (2010), 207, http://eur-lex.europa.eu/LexUriServ/LexUriServ.do?uri=CELEX:52010DC0207:EN:NOT.

18. European Global Strategy Group, "Toward a European Global Strategy: Securing European Influence in a Changing World," IAI, PISM, Elcano and UI, 2013.

19. Kalypso Nicolaidis and Rachel Kleinfield, "Rethinking Europe's 'Rule of Law' and Enlargement Agenda: The Fundamental Dilemma," OECD-EU SIGMA Paper no. 49, 2012, 14.

20. Michael Mandelbaum, *The Frugal Superpower* (New York: Public Affairs, 2010).

21. Constanze Stelzenmüller, "The West Runs Out of Power," *Policy Review* 172 (April-May 2012): 87.

22. Hillary Clinton, "The U.S. and Europe: A Revitalized Global Partnership," speech at the Brookings Institution, November 29, 2012.

23. Kagan, *The World America Made*, 75–79.

24. Daniel Hamilton and Joseph P. Quinlan, *The Transatlantic Economy 2011: Annual Survey of Jobs, Trade and Investment Between the United States and Europe* (Washington, D.C.: SAIS/Johns Hopkins, 2011), chapter 1, http://transatlantic.sais-jhu.edu/publications/books/Transatlantic_Economy_2011/te_2011.pdf.

25. Thomas Carothers, *Democracy Promotion Under Obama* (Washington, D.C.: Carnegie Endowment for International Peace, 2011).

26. Daniel Deudney and G. John Ikenberry, "Democratic Internationalism: An American Grand Strategy for a Post-Exceptionalist Era," Council on Foreign Relations Working Paper, 2012.

27. G. John Ikenberry, *Liberal Leviathan* (Princeton, N.J.: Princeton University Press, 2011), 27.

28. Graeme Herd, "The Global Puzzle: Order in an Age of Primacy, Power-Shifts and Interdependence," Geneva Papers 1, Geneva Centre for Security Policy, 2011.

29. Jean-Marc Ferry, "European Integration and the European Way," in *The European Union and Global Governance*, ed. Mario Teló (London: Routledge, 2009), 338.

30. Tzvetan Todorov, *In Defence of the Enlightenment* (London: Atlantic Books, 2010).

31. Conrad Waligorski, *Liberal Economics and Democracy* (Lawrence, Kan.: University Press of Kansas, 1997), especially chapter 7.

32. National Intelligence Council, *Global Trends 2030: Alternative Worlds* (Washington, D.C.: NIC, 2012), xiii.

33. Janis Emmanouilidis, "The Leitmotiv of a Global Europe," in *The Delphic Oracle on Europe: Is There a Future for the European Union?* eds. Loukas Tsoukalis and Janis A. Emmanouilidis (London: Oxford University Press, 2011), 193.

INDEX

Adaptive logic, 48–49

Afghanistan, 77, 94, 109

Africa, 56, 65–67. *see also specific countries*

Agency for International Development (U.S.), 117

Agenda for Action on Democracy Support (EU), 111

Agenda for Change (European Commission), 111

"Aid for trade," 56

Airbus aircraft, 71, 82–83

Air fuel taxes, 82–83

Albania, 112

Algeria, 114

Allianz Consulting, 14

Arab Spring, 113–114

Armenia, 39, 115

Arms embargo, 83

ASEAN. *see* Association of Southeast Asian Nations

Ash, Timothy Garton, 26

Ashton, Catherine, 38, 45–46, 74–76, 88–89

Asia, 43; EU relations, 5, 73–96, 117–120; financial aid, 79–80; trade relations, 59, 67, 81; U.S. relations, 73–74, 80. *see also specific countries*

Asia-Europe Meeting, 5, 74, 77, 94

Asian Development Bank, 80

Asian way, 119–120

Assad, Bashar, 114

Association of Southeast Asian Nations (ASEAN): EU relations, 68, 75–80, 86, 89–92, 118–120; Intergovernmental Commission on Human Rights, 119–120; Regional Forum, 88; Treaty of Amity and Cooperation, 75

Austria, 34, 65

Azerbaijan, 39

BAE Systems, 41, 63

Balkans, 38–39, 108, 112–113

Bangladesh, 77, 84–85

Barroso, José Manuel, 21, 43

Barysch, Katinka, 71

Beck, Ulrich, 25, 100

Belarus, 39, 116

Belgium, 34, 45

Berlusconi, Silvio, 24

Bilateralism, 126

Bilateral trade accords, 59

Bi-multilateralism, 102

Bismarckian rising powers, 121

Blake, William, 7

Bosnia, 38, 106, 109, 112–113

Brady, Hugo, 21

Brazil: defense spending, 34; EU relations, 38, 46, 63, 65, 131–132

Bremmer, Ian, 98

BRICs, 34, 38, 42, 132, 137. *see also specific countries*

Britain. *see* United Kingdom

Bundesbank, 11
Burma, 75, 117–118
Business Europe, 59, 68
Buy America campaign, 58–59
Buy European campaign, 53, 58–59

Cambodia, 75, 84–85, 119
Cameron, David, 27, 62–63, 75, 77, 119
Canada, 59, 108
Capitalism: coordinated market economy variety, 13; financialization, 54; social, 13; state, 13, 52, 54, 68–70
Carothers, Thomas, 136
Casa Árabe, 64
Caspian pipelines, 67
Caspian Sea, 67
Cecchini Report, 139
Central America, 59. *see also specific countries*
Cerny, Philip, 17, 100
Chimerica, 85
China: capitalism, 64; defense spending, 34; economic power, 11, 15–17, 27, 82, 99; EU relations, 5, 53, 56, 61–67, 76–95, 118–119, 133–134, 139; exports, 78; financial aid, 103; global relations, 101; nationalism, 82–83; trade relations, 58, 78; U.S. relations, 75, 91–94
China Investment Corporation, 79, 85
Chinese Communist Party, 92
Citizenship rights, 118
Civil Society Forum (EaP), 114–116
Clinton, Hillary, 135–136
"Cloak and dagger" protectionism, 58
Code of Conduct for Pooling and Sharing, 45
Colombia, 59
Commercial diplomacy, 60–65
Commercial expansion, 53
Common Foreign and Security Policy (EU), 43
Common Security and Defense Policy (CSDP) (EU), 34, 46, 105–106
Compensation, 46
Competence struggles, 127
Competitiveness, 15

Core questions, 3–6
Cosmopolitanism, 100
Côte d'Ivoire, 106, 109
Crisis management, 1–6, 9–30, 42–50, 124–129
Croatia, 112
Crouch, Colin, 18–19
CSDP. *see* Common Security and Defense Policy
Cyprus, 12, 18–19, 33, 117
Czech Republic, 28, 45, 110

Dalai Lama, 77, 83, 118–119
Danone, 55
Deep and Comprehensive Free Trade Area Agreements (DCFTA), 115
Deficit trends, 11–12
De Gucht, Karel, 55, 80
Democracy: crisis of, 23, 125; liberal, 24; post-democracy, 18–19; support for, 22–23, 29, 108–112, 119–120
Democratic cooperation, 131–132
Democratic internationalism, 136
Democratic legitimacy, 18–24
Denmark, 34, 64, 71, 77, 110
Development aid, 35
Diplomacy: commercial, 60–65; economic, 64, 76; network, 28; nuclear, 92; raw materials, 58
Dirty trade war, 87
Doha Round, 69–70

EADS, 41
EAS, 36, 45–46
Eastern Partnership (EaP), 114–116; Civil Society Forum, 114–115
Eastern states, 114–116
ECB. *see* European Central Bank
Economic crisis, 9–30, 42–49; legacy of, 124–129; as opportunity, 49–50; as silver-lined, 42
Economic diplomacy, 51–52, 64, 76
Economic growth, 12, 14
Economic policy, 29
Economist, 15, 40, 52, 58–59
EED. *see* European Endowment for Democracy

Egypt, 114
EIDHR, 111
Eliot, T. S., 1
Elitism, 23
Engagement Plan (EU-Pakistan), 76, 89
Engineers, 15
ESDP, 111
Estonia, 34
EU2020, 15, 69
EU-China Strategic Dialogue, 88–89
EU-China Strategic Partnership, 83–84
Eurasia Group, 52
Euro, 33
Eurofighter jets, 63
Euro-nationalism, 25
Europa, 50
Europe: Chinese investment in, 77; crisis
    of survival, 49; engineers, 15; financial
    aid, 79; geoeconomic, 51–72; global,
    31–50, 123–140; market power, 37;
    patent system, 15; renationalization of,
    40; social protection spending, 12; stra-
    tegic partnerships, 5; as trading state,
    54; two-belief, 40; venture capital, 15.
    see also specific countries
European Central Bank (ECB), 11–12,
    18–19, 33, 56, 60
European Citizens' Initiative, 21
European Commission: Agenda for
    Change, 111; Asia relations, 77; crisis
    management, 12, 15, 24; financial aid,
    80; foreign policy, 43, 133; geoeco-
    nomics, 54, 67; Global Europe 2050,
    21; global relations, 109; Governance
    Initiative, 110–111; subcommittees,
    135; trade policy, 57
European Commission Task Force on
    Defense Industries and Markets, 45
European Council on Foreign Relations,
    36
European Court of Justice, 19
European Defense Agency, 45
European Economic Area, 47
European Endowment for Democracy
    (EED), 111–112
European External Action Service, 43
European Global Strategy, 44, 108

European Institute for Peace, 46
European Instrument for Democracy and
    Human Rights, 110
Europeanization, 134–135
European Neighborhood Policy, 35
European Parliament, 19, 23, 35
European Security Strategy, 41
European Stability Mechanism, 79
European Union (EU): as adjustment
    union, 12; Agenda for Action on De-
    mocracy Support, 111; arms embargo,
    83; ASEAN relations, 68, 75–80, 86,
    89–92, 118–120; Asia relations, 5,
    73–96, 117–120; Caspian pipelines
    strategy, 67; Common Foreign and
    Security Policy, 43; Common Security
    and Defense Policy (CSDP), 34, 46,
    105–106; competitiveness budget, 15;
    crisis management, 1–6, 9–30, 42–50,
    124–129; defense spending, 34–35, 90;
    democracy problem, 125; development
    aid, 35; as disunited, 39–42; economic
    crisis, 1–6, 9–30, 42–50, 124–129;
    economic policy, 66; financial aid,
    79; foreign direct investment, 32–33;
    foreign policy, 1–2, 6, 40–41, 97,
    112–120, 125–140; future directions,
    6–7; German hegemony over, 25–28;
    global relations, 2–4, 32–33, 36; influ-
    ence by example, 48; innovation policy,
    16; as insurance union, 12; integration
    of, 42–44; international policy, 3–5;
    legacy of crisis, 124–129; as liberal
    power, 97; multilateralism, 102–105;
    New Asia Strategy, 74; paradox of
    politics, 46; as political union, 18–24;
    power after attraction, 36–39; power-
    by-attraction, 4, 37; protectionism,
    55–56; research expenditures, 15; secu-
    rity policy, 105–108; social capitalism,
    13; social market model, 10; Strategic
    Framework and Action Plan on Human
    Rights and Democracy, 111; strategic
    partnerships, 5; Structural Funds, 16;
    structure, 44–46; support for democra-
    cy, 22–23, 29, 108–112, 119–120; trade
    policy, 55–59; trade relations, 32–33,

54–55, 59, 81, 86–87; U.S. relations, 59, 86–87, 91–92, 136–137
"Europe a Prophecy" (Blake), 7
Euro plus, 28
Eurozone, 79
Eurozone crisis, 1–6, 9–30, 124–129
Exceptionalism, 136
External Action Service, 35–36, 78, 105

FDI. *see* Foreign direct investment
Feldstein, Martin, 39–40
Ferguson, Niall, 100
Financial aid, 79–80
Financial crisis, 9–30, 42–49; legacy of, 124–129; as opportunity, 49–50; as silver-lined, 42
Financialization, 54
Fischer, Joschka, 40
Flexibility, 46–47
Flexi-lateralism, 103–104
Foreign direct investment (FDI), 32–33, 61, 76
Foreign policy, 35–36, 40–41, 45–46, 49–50, 128, 137–140; globalization of, 64–65
France: Asia relations, 75, 89–90; commercial diplomacy, 64; defense spending, 34–35; and economic crisis, 12–17, 20–21; foreign policy, 41, 46–47, 106–107, 114; funds to multilateral bodies, 104; global relations, 41, 43, 103; protectionism, 55; support for democracy, 110, 131; trade policy, 57, 68; UK relations, 45–46, 107
Frankfurt Group, 28
Free trade, 59, 67, 90–91
Future directions, 6–7
Future of Europe Group, 127

Gazprom, 116
Gbagbo, Laurent, 109
Generalized System of Preferences (GSP), 56
Geoeconomics, 51–72
Geopolitics, 107
Georgia, 39, 115–116

Germany: arms exports, 61; Asia relations, 75; China relations, 81–82, 93; defense budget, 34; development aid, 35; and economic crisis, 3, 10–15, 19–21; foreign policy, 27, 46–47; geoeconomic power, 61, 65–67; global relations, 41–46, 62, 103, 106–107, 112–116, 125, 132–133; hegemony, 25–28; support for democracy, 109; trade policy, 58, 61, 81–82
Giddens, Anthony, 17, 134
Global human rights. *see* Human rights
Globalization: of foreign policy, 64–65; management of, 48
Global middle class, 70
Global relations, 101; European influence on, 31–50; redesigning, 123–140
Global Trade Alert, 55, 58
Governance Initiative (European Commission), 110–111
Gowan, Richard, 36
Grass, Günter, 26
Gray, John, 18
Greece: development aid, 35; economic crisis, 10–12, 24; foreign policy, 41, 47, 113
Grevi, Giovanni, 38
Growth discourse, 14
Guanglie, Liang, 88–89
Gulf states, 33, 48, 63
Gulf Union, 48

Hague, William, 62, 75
Hawk jets, 63
Hegemony, German, 25–28
Held, David, 100
Helm, Dieter, 17–18
High-Level Economic and Trade Dialogue, 87
Hill, Steven, 13
Hollande, François, 12–13, 15, 26–27, 55, 64, 106
Horizontality, 21–22
Howorth, Jolyon, 133
Human rights, 104, 109–111, 118
Human Rights Watch, 23
Hungary, 23–24, 28, 45

Idealism, 137
Ikenberry, John, 99
IMF. *see* International Monetary Fund
Imperialism, liberal, 130
India, 15, 76–78; defense spending, 34;
    EU relations, 63–65, 86, 89, 94–95,
    131–132, 139; financial aid, 35, 79;
    funds to multilateral bodies, 104
Indonesia, 56, 75, 77, 84–85, 131–132
Infrastructure projects, 15
Innovation, 16
Innovation Union initiative, 16
Institute of International Finance, 33
Integration logic, 43–44
Intergovernmental Commission on Hu-
    man Rights (ASEAN), 119–120
International Court of Justice, 104
International Institute of Democracy and
    Election Management, 132
Internationalism, 136
International Labor Organization, 118
International Monetary Fund (IMF),
    11–12, 33, 79–80, 103, 105
Interventionism, partial, 60
Iran, 114
Ireland, 34, 63
Italy: Asia strategy, 88; defense budget,
    34; economic crisis, 11–12, 17, 24;
    economic diplomacy, 64; foreign policy,
    107; funds to multilateral bodies, 104;
    geoeconomics, 65; global relations,
    43–45, 108

Jackson, Tim, 17–18
Jacques, Martin, 81, 98
Japan, 76, 78, 93–94; EU relations, 88–90,
    92; financial aid, 79; support for de-
    mocracy, 108
Joffe, Josef, 28–29
Jordan, 114
Juan Carlos, 64

Kagan, Robert, 123
Kazakhstan, 61, 64
Khanna, Parag, 53
King, Stephen, 52–53
Kosovo, 38, 113

Krastev, Ivan, 22
Kundnani, Hans, 82
Kupchan, Charles, 98

Labour Party, 62
Laos, 75
Laqueur Walter, 49
Latin America, 66–67
Lebanon, 106, 114
Legitimacy, democratic, 18–24
Lehmann, Jean-Pierre, 69
Leonard, Mark, 98
Letta, Enrico, 17
Liberal democracy, 24
Liberal imperialism, 130
Liberal internationalism, 136
Liberalism, 21–22; humbled adjustment,
    137–140; multipolar, 129–137
Liberal peace-building, 107
Liberal realism, 128
Liberal world order, 97–121
Libya, 106, 109, 113–114
Liddle, Roger, 17
Lisbon Treaty, 21, 40–41, 61, 105, 127
London School of Economics, 100
Luxembourg, 45

Macedonia, 113
Magnitsky, Sergei, 117
Mahbubani, Kishore, 74
Malaysia, 65, 76, 78
Mali, 105–106
Mallaby, Sebastian, 12
Marca España (Trademark Spain), 64
Market competitiveness, 15
Market fundamentalism, 13
Market intervention, 60–61
Market power Europe, 37
Marsh, David, 25–26
Menon, Anand, 46
Mercantilism, 70
Mercosur, 67
Merkel, Angela, 11–12, 19–20, 25, 27, 41,
    61, 116, 118
Mexico, 38
Middle East, 66, 113–114. *see also specific*
    countries

Military structure, 43
Minilateralism, 120–121
Modernization, 117
Moïsi, Dominique, 47
Moldova, 39, 108, 115–116
Mongolia, 61
Monnet method, 23
Montenegro, 112
Monti, Mario, 57
Moravcsik, Andrew, 24
Morocco, 65, 114
Moyo, Dambisa, 53
Multiculturalism, 129
Multilateralism, 66–67, 120–121, 134;
    bi-multilateralism, 102; gate-keeping,
    102–105
Multipolar liberalism, 129–137

Nabucco project, 67
National Intelligence Council, 139
Nationalism: euro-nationalism, 25; rena-
    tionalization, 40; supranationalism,
    28–29
NATO. see North Atlantic Treaty Orga-
    nization
Neighborhood Civil Society Facility,
    114–115
Neo-functionalism, 43
Neoliberalism, 13
Nepal, 77
Netherlands: commercial diplomacy, 64;
    defense budget, 34; development aid,
    35; economic crisis, 14; geoeconomics,
    66–67; global relations, 45; support
    for democracy, 109, 111; trade policy,
    57–58
Network diplomacy, 28
New Asia Strategy, 74
NGOs. see Nongovernmental organiza-
    tions
Niger, 105
Nongovernmental organizations (NGOs),
    35
North Atlantic Treaty Organization
    (NATO), 44–45, 107
North Korea, 89, 92
Nuclear diplomacy, 92

Nuclear power, 46
Nye, Joseph, 128

Obama, Barack, 58–59, 136
OECD. see Organization for Economic
    Cooperation and Development
Offshoring, 56
Open Government Partnership, 131
Orban, Viktor, 23
Organization for Economic Cooperation
    and Development (OECD), 10
Osborne, George, 63, 77
Overseas Development Institute, 84

Pacifism, 107
Pakistan, 76, 89, 94–95
Paradox of politics, 46
Parello-Plesner, Jonas, 71, 82, 91
Parochialism, 82, 127
Partial interventionism, 60
Partnership and Cooperation Agreements,
    90–91
Patents, 15
Peace-building, 107
Peru, 59
Philippines, 76, 78, 84–85
Piebalgs, Andris, 118
Pisani-Ferry, Jean, 40
Plurilateralism, 68
Poland: aid to, 110; defense spending, 34;
    economic crisis, 27; foreign policy,
    64–65, 114–115, 117; global relations,
    43–45, 107–108; support for democ-
    racy, 111
Policy without politics, 22
Political partnerships, 87–95
Portugal, 12
Post-democracy, 18–19
Power-by-attraction, 4, 37
Power reversal, 78–84
Power shifts, 25–28, 132–134; after attrac-
    tion, 36–39; reversal, 78–84
Protectionism, 55–56, 58
Provincialism, 40
Putin, Vladimir, 116–117

Rafale jets, 65

Raw materials diplomacy, 58
Realism: defensive structural, 99; liberal, 128; rise and fall, 98
Reciprocity, 56–59
Reform-liberalism, 13
Renationalization, 40
Renault, 64
Research expenditures, 15
Re-shoring, 56
"Responsibility to protect" concept, 132
"Responsibility while protecting" concept, 132
Rise and fall realism, 98
Rosecrance, Richard, 43
Rover, 77
Russia: defense spending, 34; geoeconomics, 38, 63; global relations, 33, 101, 116–117
Rutte, Mark, 64
Rwanda, 109

Saab, 77
Saakashvili, Mikheil, 116
Salafis, 114
Sarkozy, Nicolas, 27, 79, 83
Saudi Arabia, 34, 63–64
Schmidt, Vivien, 22
Security, 44–45, 105–108
Serbia, 38, 112
Shangri-La Dialogue, 88
Siemens, 65
Sikorski, Radosław, 26
Singapore issues, 55
Skidelsky, Robert, 13, 53
Slovakia, 45, 110
Social capitalism, 13
Social-liberalism, 13
Social market model, 10
Social protection spending, 12
Somalia, 105
Soros, George, 25
South Africa, 65, 90, 131–132
South Korea, 59, 76, 89, 131
Spain: defense spending, 34–35; development aid, 35, 79–80; economic crisis, 10–11, 15–16, 27; exports, 64; foreign policy, 64, 107; funds to multilateral

bodies, 104; global relations, 43–44, 108; protectionism, 55; trade policy, 57
Speck, Ulrich, 107
Sri Lanka, 84–85
State capitalism, 13, 52, 54, 70
Stephens, Philip, 26, 62
Stiglitz, Joseph, 13
Strategic Framework and Action Plan on Human Rights and Democracy (EU), 111
Strategic liberalization, 60
Strategic partnerships, 5
Strategy for Smart, Sustainable and Inclusive Growth (EU2020), 15, 69
Sub-Saharan Africa, 66–67. *see also specific countries*
Supranationalism, 28–29
Suu Kyi, Aung San, 118
Sweden: development aid, 35; economic crisis, 28; global relations, 44, 108; support for democracy, 110–111
Swieboda, Pawel, 29, 48
Syria, 106, 109, 113–114

Taiwan, 76, 78
Taiwan Strait, 94
TAP. *see* Trans Adriatic Pipeline
TGF, 65
Thailand, 56, 76
Thames Water, 77
Tibet, 83
Touareg, 106
Trade relations, 32–33, 54–59, 67–68, 87
Trans Adriatic Pipeline (TAP), 65
Transatlanticism, post-hegemonic, 135–137
Transatlantic Trade and Investment Partnership (TTIP), 59, 68
Trans-institutionalism, 133
Transnistria, 116
Trans-Pacific Partnership, 91
Treaty of Amity and Cooperation (ASEAN), 75
Tsoukalis, Loukas, 26
TTIP. *see* Transatlantic Trade and Investment Partnership

Turkey: democratic advance, 108; development aid, 35; global relations, 38, 41, 47, 131–132
Turkmenistan, 67
Tusk, Donald, 117
Tymoshenko, Yulia, 115
Typhoon fighters, 63, 65

UAE. *see* United Arab Emirates
UK. *see* United Kingdom
Ukraine, 39, 108, 115–116
United Arab Emirates (UAE), 63, 71
United Kingdom (UK), 28; Asia relations, 75–76, 88–90; "Capability, Accountability and Responsiveness" framework, 109; cooperation with France, 45–46, 107; defense spending, 34–35; development aid, 35, 77; economic crisis, 13, 20–21, 26–28; exports, 63; fiscal deficit, 107; flexibility, 46–47; foreign policy, 41, 46, 62, 114; legacy of crisis, 124; protectionism, 55; support for democracy, 109, 131; trade policy, 57–58, 63, 67, 69, 71, 77
United National Movement, 116
United Nations, 104
United Nations Democracy Fund, 104
United Nations Development Program, 60
United States (U.S.): Asia relations, 73–75, 80, 88, 90–91, 95–96; China relations, 78, 91–94; crisis of democracy, 23; economic strategy, 11, 13; EU relations, 59, 86–87, 91–92, 136–137; foreign

policy, 112–113, 135–137; liberal internationalism, 136; neoliberalism, 13; support for democracy, 108, 131; trade relations, 59, 86–87
Universalism, 99
U.S. *see* United States

Van Middelaar, Luuk, 42
Van Rompuy, Herman, 19, 42, 54, 117, 119, 127
Venture capital, 15
Vietnam, 75–78, 84–85, 91, 119
Volvo, 77

Wall, Peter, 107
Westerwelle, Guido, 27, 32–33, 88
Wolf, Martin, 12
Woolcock, Stephen, 55
World Bank, 17, 79–80
World order(s): eclectic, 98–101; liberal, 97–121
World Trade Organization (WTO), 53, 56, 58–59, 86, 104

Yanukovych, Viktor, 115
Year of Asia, 74
Yemen, 35, 113–114
Yeo Lay Hwee, 90
Yollies, 15

Zapatero, José Luis Rodríguez, 79
Zhimin, Chen, 85–86
Zimbabwe, 35

ABOUT THE AUTHOR

Richard Youngs is a senior associate at Carnegie Europe and is part of the Carnegie Endowment's Democracy and Rule of Law Program. He is also a professor of international relations at the University of Warwick. Prior to joining Carnegie in July 2013, he was director of the Madrid- and Brussels-based think tank FRIDE. Youngs also held positions in the UK Foreign and Commonwealth Office and as an EU Marie Curie fellow, and he was a senior fellow at the Transatlantic Academy in Washington, DC, from 2012 to 2013. He has written six previous books on different aspects of the EU's international policies.

CARNEGIE EUROPE

Founded in 2007, **Carnegie Europe** is the European center of the Carnegie Endowment for International Peace. From its newly expanded presence in Brussels, Carnegie Europe combines the work of its research platform with the fresh perspectives of Carnegie's centers in Washington, Moscow, Beijing, and Beirut, bringing a unique global vision to the European policy community. Through publications, articles, seminars, and private consultations, Carnegie Europe aims to foster new thinking on the daunting international challenges shaping Europe's role in the world.

***

The **Carnegie Endowment for International Peace** is a unique global network of policy research centers in Russia, China, Europe, the Middle East, and the United States. Our mission, dating back more than a century, is to advance the cause of peace through analysis and development of fresh policy ideas and direct engagement and collaboration with decisionmakers in government, business, and civil society. Working together, our centers bring the inestimable benefit of multiple national viewpoints to bilateral, regional, and global issues.